1

English Brexit

By

Paul Thind

About the author

Dr. Paul Thind was born into a traditional Sikh family on January 1, 1955 in a small village, Mohie, in the Punjab. Aged 11, in 1965 he was brought to Ealing, London. Against the odds and thanks to free education, he went to University of East Anglia and gained a PhD in Chemistry.

From a young age, Paul was fascinated by science. After reading Origin of Species by Charles Darwin, Paul increasingly distanced himself from Sikhism and God, preferring instead to believe in Einstein and his theories of Relativity.

His first job was in Minnesota, USA at 3M as a Research Scientist. Five years later, then married, the family moved back to London and Dr. Thind changed professions to become a banker. In time his area of speciality became trading and risk management of credit and derivatives portfolios. Dr. Thind worked several financial institutions including Deutsche Bank, UBS, ABN AMRO, RBS and HSBC during his 30-years. The family, with three young children, moved to Zurich, Switzerland in 1992. The children went to Swiss schools.

In recent years Paul Thind worked as a consultant and for periods lived in Vienna, Hong Kong, Singapore and Sydney.

Paul Thind retired in 2017.

Paul Thind has self-published three works. Displaced, Rebirth and English Brexit. All, in some respects, view the world from the outside – how little of who we are or what we become is planned or predictable – how impossible it is to shed the baggage and burdens of our individual histories.

Paul spends his time primarily in London, Switzerland, and India.

PREFACE

I started writing this book in 2016 as the Brexit debates were heating up in Great Britain. At the time I was living in Sydney, Australia. Watching the rancour and divisions in my country was heart-breaking. The familiar extremist voices from a distant past of the 1960s and 1970s echoed in my mind. This time Great Britain was split along many lines. The less well-educated, the old, the North voted to Leave. The better educated, the South East, the young on the whole voted to Remain.

Scotland and N. Ireland were pro EU. Wales and England voted to leave. The Tories had elected Mrs. Theresa May as the party's leader. The Conservatives were in power but without an overall majority. A bargain, cash for votes, had been struck with the DUP in Ireland which allowed the government to function. Labour had Jeremy Corbyn as the leader, who was ambivalent about the EU, while majority of the Labour party members were Remainers. The Labour party could only be effective with the support of the SNP, The Green Party, and the Lib Dems.

Nigel Farage had emerged as the undisputed voice of the Brexiters. There were enough votes among his supporters to make the difference between winning and losing the next election.

America had elected Donald Trump as its President. Mr. Trump promoted his ultra-nationalist agenda, often voicing anti-German or anti-EU rhetoric. This encouraged not only the English nationalists but also the *AltRight* in Germany, Le Pen in France, Victor Orbán in Hungary, Matteo Salvini and others. The wave of nationalism was in full swing.

The ever-increasing poison of the Far-Right Tories and Nigel Farage followers made me fear that something far more sinister could result. Boris Johnson had referred to black people as piccaninnies and people with watermelon smiles. I questioned what was driving this new fascist movement. What were the origins of English nationalism? How would it impact the nation? Were we, as victors of the great wars, going back to a tragic era when the Nazis were dominant in Europe? Why were we willing to give up Free Movement and Tariff Free Trade?

From 2011 to 2014 I had lived in Hong Kong and Singapore. I was impressed by the living standards and the efficiency of those economic systems. I noticed the inequalities also. In particular, the cruel labour laws. Economically, as former colonies of Great Britain, these small countries had overtaken Britain in many respects. The questions I had been asking was: Could Britain achieve similar success unchained and outside the EU? What would have to be sacrificed? Would the EU tolerate a Singapore next door?

I was trying to answer many questions. On my visits back to England, I encountered, purely by accident, a few Brexiters. As I started to talk to them, I was shocked by how they felt about Europe and the EU. Other than boozing holidays in Spain, none of them had lived or experienced Europe. Yet, they hated 'them' so much. Some still longed for that long-gone era of British colonialism. They objected to being 'dictated to' by Brussels. They talked about having lost 'Sovereignty' and wanted to take back control of their country and control its borders.

England, the country I grew up in and had made my own, was becoming increasingly unrecognisable. Our politicians lied and misled the public. The newspapers spread untruths and our gullible public didn't fact check. Anger, abuse and emotion was their only rebuttal. Social media compounded the divisions.

Brexit, in my view, is an act of withdrawal and an act of national self-harm. The consequences will impact our lives for generations and will reduce our potential as individuals and as a nation.

4

I am conscious of the fact that the title of this work and the content will offend many. But we are defined by the choices our nation makes. In a democracy the behaviour of the majority impacts the lives of all. We can't isolate ourselves from our neighbours, our friends or the people who live in the regions. If there is a majority of Brexiters in Great Britain, that reflects on us all. If your neighbour is a racist and you do not nothing, you are complicit. If there is sex or gender discrimination in our country, we are all to blame.

I am who I am because I was raised in England. I am not blind to our virtues or failings. In writing this book, my wish is for us to look around, observe and ask questions. What kind of a nation are we a part of? Are we on the right path? Is this what we want for our children?

What shapes us?

What is the mindset of a people whose forefathers ruled a quarter of the world's people and a lot more of the Earth's total area? Britain invaded and ruled over more than three quarters of the world's countries in its history. To state that Great Britain was the world's most powerful country by far, at its peak, is not an understatement. The British empire was much bigger than the Roman Empire and some might argue even more influential.

One cannot blame even the ordinary people of this great nation, to think that the world is their oyster, and they have a special place in it. People from all backgrounds and nations try to lift their spirits by glorifying their special personal past. No one can question the historical significance of Great Britain. How many of us are willing to accept the current reality and the future that is unfolding? What will be our place in the world?

Why am I writing this? Who am I to have the right to make pronouncements about what should happen in England or Great Britain?

I am a British Citizen of Indian descent. I am a first-generation immigrant. I am not English. But I know the English, in some respects, better than they know themselves. I have experienced their hate and their love, like a welcomed stepson to a mother, and a competitor to the other siblings. England and Great Britain are now mine and I belong to it. The English, the Scots, the Irish and the Welsh are mine and I am now of this soil.

My father came to England in 1963 when I was 9 years old. My father had a strong connection to Great Britain. He fought in the WWII and in December 1945 he was sent to London to participate in the victory celebrations.

When we were young, my father told us stories of his time in the army and during the war. His best friend was drowned off the coast of Tripoli when the Germans sank the ship he was on. Others had died in battles in North Africa or in Burma. The fact that his life was spared turned him into a staunch believer in his God and made him humble.

He understood that our destiny as individuals is shaped by events that are often not in our control. He told us that even great leaders such as Winston Churchill often were swept by events and were reacting to what was unfolding rather than shaping the future. Hitler was happening to them and something mad was obviously happening to Hitler which caused millions of lives to be lost and millions more maimed or made useless by war. The hard-fought victory then also shaped us and the way we interact with each other. I also grew up hating Hitler. The Second World War is thus also part of my personal history. Through my father's contributions it is a victory I can legitimately celebrate. My father helped to preserve our freedoms, our democracy, and our way of life in England. An England that has a rich tapestry of which I too am a part of.

My father's time and shared observations has shaped my own relationship with England and Great Britain. I feel I have a unique stake in this country because even though he saw himself as a small pawn in the great effort to attain victory over Hitler and the Japanese, I know that without that collective effort the war would have been lost and the world would be quite different today. The loss of 6 million Jewish lives tells us about the scale of madness. Millions of lives sacrificed by the Allied forces and citizens of the Commonwealth brings home the scale of the tragedy.

I have a stake in England, in the United Kingdom and Europe. I have given my all and planted my own seed and invested in my vision of Europe. We identify ourselves as British – but are obviously not English. My children describe themselves as people of Indian origin who were born in England. Brexit will impact their lives even more than mine. They are citizens in equal measure. Their hopes, dreams and even their fears are linked to the success or failure of England and how the countries of the United Kingdom will evolve.

The enduring lesson of WWII, my father often told me, is that for once Great Britain, the colonies and of course the Allied nations were on the right side of history. Hitler was, we all know, an evil man. The German people connived with this treacherous person to cause misery and racial hatred on a scale unimaginable. My own first impressions of the suffering were formed watching the BBC's recount of the war and images of concentration camps and then later reading the accounts of Anne Frank and others. Having heard the stories from my father the sadness that humanity can sink to such inhumane depths touched me at an early age and sometimes still haunts.

When I first arrived in England aged 11 with a turban on my head and long hair, I was not made to feel welcomed. At school we fought with the English boys who taunted us and told us to go home. 'We are here to collect our dues,' I used to retort. 'You have taken everything from our country and now we are here to take something back.' I did not know then that we were not going to take anything back at all. But I do remember feeling odd saying those things. Even then the words rang hollow. We knew that we were never going to go back. I did not know then that England would be forever our new home and our new country. I did not know then that as I got to know my new country, I would fall in love not just with England, but also Wales, Scotland, and Ireland. I did not know then that in time I would overcome in most cases the obstacles of white English boys and win them over as friends – at least the ones I wanted to be friends with.

What we did know was that going back to India was not a prospect. By hook or by crook we were going to find our feet and establish long term roots. We had to overcome racism. We had to fight and confront racism and bigotry every day.

Sometimes our arguments led to fist fights. I was not particularly good at fist fighting. But I had played *kabaddi* as a kid and I was fortunately quite fast. I had come from the farm. These were pale City boys. With boys of my size and age I do not ever remember losing a physical fight. But in life there is always someone bigger and stronger that one must deal with. I soon discovered that the way to deal with big is to call them out for what they are. When someone big picked on me, from time to time I had sympathy from others. Someone would shout out: 'Pick someone of your own size!' That was often relief if the bully backed off. Or I would challenge them at something different. 'You might be stronger than me, but I can run faster than you!' I might say to distract. Or when all was lost, I would say, 'Let me fight someone my size.' But it was humiliating to know that size alone can result in one being made to feel weak or subservient. Subservience, however, was not part of our makeup. 'Sikhs are brave,' I had been told all my conscious life. 'You don't back down. You do not come home crying. You have to face the bullies.'

I knew that there were boys my size who were stronger. But luckily for me no one ever came forward to challenge me. There was a lesson to be learnt about the English boys. Not all were bullies, and most had been taught by their parent's certain values about fairness. They could see that I was alone and even when they were being goaded to pick a fight with me because I was a foreigner, they did not always bite.

But once a fight started, no one tried to stop it. Instead, the English form a ring around the two opponents. It is like a boxing ring made of a chanting mob. The English leave room for a 'fair' fight and allow it to run to its conclusion. They want to establish and know the picking order. I was thus lucky in some respects. Even though I was the one being victimised, I felt good after each win. I knew I had gained some respect.

Of course, it was not the same for everyone. Racism is experienced differently by each person encountering it. The English are either silent when observing the suffering of others or they are relentless and have no pity whatsoever. They can continue to inflict wounds long after a person or a nation is down. The English tend to reduce their opponents to helplessness. To a place of retreat from which they cannot easily or quickly recover. I suppose that is how they ruled the world.

Sitting in that classroom and standing around in the freezing cold during breaks, drinking free milk, it took time to make friends and understand my enemies.

I spent several years learning English. Not knowing the language was a form of segregation. Segregation comes in many forms. It can be forced on one by the host community through separation of colours and classes. In England, this form of segregation was apparent to me as I walked past a Grammar School each day. Those kids knew that we were walking up from our Secondary School past their Grammar School and were going to the same train station. We knew that we were at a worse school, where the chances of going into higher education were reduced. Those Grammar School kids appeared to be better behaved, better dressed and they had an air of snobbery about them. There were fewer black kids among them. In those days also fewer Asians. We were the first generation of children to arrive in the early 1960's. In my own family the age range varied from 8 to 18 when our parents brought us to England. The eldest spoke a bit of English. I only knew ABC on arrival. But I knew by heart my multiplication tables to 20X20, which was not the case with First Form kids at school.

I remember well suffering a little bit from being segregated because I wore a turban, and my skin was not pale white. I also remember the segregation of the different school uniforms and the knowledge we were in a different league altogether because in our school we had all the kids who had failed their 11-plus. We were put into different lanes with reduced chances. I felt like the servants we had employed in India. I was conscious of the fact that their lives did not count as much. I felt bitter that I was not allowed to go to the best schools.

Segregation at school also happened first thing in the morning. We could skip Assembly because they sang Christian hymns, and the Headmaster gave a sermon at the end of it. We were excused because the school recognised that we were from a different faith. Perhaps that was the time when I first started to question faith itself as it dawned on me that we were excluding ourselves and were being excluded. It was an uncomfortable condition even at the age of eleven or twelve.

Of course, there was the primitive form of segregation as it was exercised in the United States and many White Ruled African countries. Another form of segregation is self-imposed. That is where people withdraw from potential friends, potential loves, potential prospects to be able to contribute to society and even more damaging, they withdraw and reduce their own prospects to lead better lives. Both come at a great economic cost to the country. But I digress.

As we learnt our maths, played games, and sat in class, inevitably we were also learning to accept each other. Books are always the great leveller. But having experienced discrimination the mistrust between myself and English boys persisted for years. One could not tell by simply looking at a white person if he or she was or not a racist. To me they all looked the same and until one interacted one could not deduce anything. Even knowing that they were not all the same the suspicions prevented one from interacting with strangers.

When one looks around the globe one can see that Britain has been one of the most civilised and civilising places in the world. So much so that people exploit the great freedoms that are meant to be our virtues. The freedom of expression or Free Speech, the freedom to worship the God of our choosing, the freedom to belong to any form of political organisation (except terrorist organisation). We are constantly striving for greater equality and to give freedom to gender diversity. Even though the struggles have been long, and the full measure of equality still eludes us in 2019. Discrimination between the different ethnic groups is still a curse in our society. It was much worse in the 1960's. Racism was much more entrenched at the time. In parts of the UK it is still entrenched. In parts that have been left behind, where traditional industries have closed, and new investments were not directed by successive governments. Places where people were never able to save enough to start own businesses or even to be able to migrate to Australia, Canada, United States or New Zealand. Deprived of a good education, deprived of hard skills, unable to speak German, Swedish, Dutch etc. they certainly found it hard to move to thriving parts of Europe; although if they had the resources they would have discovered that speaking only English would be sufficient to find jobs, when there were none in the Midlands.

Our classroom was the first place that brought our differences to focus. It was also the classroom that started to break down the barriers and replace distrust with respect for each other. I learnt that differences must be brought into focus through some form of debate or confrontation to narrow the gap.

When we had open debates, when we shouted, screamed and confronted each other, simple humanity, intelligence, and reason usually won. Pain and fighting in the playground also led to progress. Hate could not persist because we had to interact. Sooner or later even dumb people see that common humanity unites us more compared with superficial differences. Hurt is common to us all. When I was called a 'wog' I hurt. When I called them 'white pigs' I am sure they too were upset.

Even in my Secondary Modern School we had some very bright white kids. Kids who did not perpetuate hate, who did not rise to the bait when the thugs were leading them on. Knowing where I came from, I was not sure how we would treat strangers. Because Britain had ruled over us, we had unspoken respect for white people. I did not know then that it took only a few white men to rule nations with populations of millions. I did not know as a child that our people had been complicit in the white man's colonisation of our country. At the time, a part of me felt that perhaps as people the English were superior. Their success, the Empire, had clearly rubbed on them. They had a right to assume that they were a superior race. The knowledge that they had the biggest empire in human history must have made the British an immensely proud people.

When I saw the class structure, the divisions between workers and employers, I was not so sure that this great civilization was any different from the caste system we had left behind. I was not so sure that the white boys in my class had any right to look down upon me. In some respects, I looked down on them.

I remember a white lad telling me once that he belonged to God's chosen people - chosen to lead, chosen to have dominion over others. I remember asking myself who had planted that message in his head. I imagined his father talking to him and convincing him how special he was simply because he was born as an Englishman. In succeeding years, I realised that even some of the poor working classes, even with snoot running from their noses thought that they were somehow a 'special' race. Our history can lead us to many personal shores. Some real, some totally delusional. There I was with a big turban on my head, thinking I was the king. I was special. I was the liberator.

When I was growing up my parents told me of the times before India's partition when they lived in Lahore, Pakistan. My grandfather worked as catering manager in some compound of white people. He was head of purchasing and planning. Apparently, it was a well-paid job and had its side benefits. My mother told us about Mam Sahibs with their floating hair and milk white skins. She made it sound even romantic. My father was more circumspect. He had his war experiences before 1945 and then had witnessed the lead up to independence and the mass migration and violence. He knew what the British were capable of. Despite that his love for humanity and to being able to treat men, even great men as mere mortals who bled just as much, hurt just as much prevented him from putting white people on any pedestal. On the battlefield, at the front line all men are equal. My father had lived that equality and had looked white men eye to eye and had measured them. He had concluded that they were not any different. White people were not more agile, not more knowledgeable, or smarter, not braver, not more emotional, not stronger and were equally fragile.

I knew that with many of my classmates, their individual lives were better than ours. It did not matter if their individual habits were worse. It did not matter if their individual values were inferior. Irrespective, in a sense, secretly I admired the English and wanted to be more like them. As a collection, as a nation, England was at a different place compared with India, the country we had left behind. The country we had to leave behind out of necessity and natural human desire to optimise our circumstances. Perhaps in even better circumstances we would have left. Later in life, I also left Britain for altogether different reasons. For adventure, for the unknown. Not out of necessity but to live a fuller life, a better quality of life and to simply be among strangers, to explore, to optimise. Those too are human traits. To walk into the wilderness to see what is over the hills or across the deserts and oceans. We are creatures of the planet, not of a place. Migration is part of our makeup.

As time passed and I experienced life at school and walked the streets and played sports and argued and cried I obviously saw that not all English people were superior. Perhaps none were. They were just people. Some wealthier, some taller, some better educated, some with better physiques. Some had disabilities like everyone else. Many drank and smoked, which was a low-class habit in our culture. When either school kids or at school our teacher smoked, we did not think very much of them. We felt that they were filthy. If they smoked, we were not entirely sure if they bathed regularly. We heard that many homes did not have hot water. It was revelation to me that there were public places where people went to bathe once a week. I had come from a place where we awoke at 5 am and drew water from a well and bathed each morning.

There were poor people and disabled people in England just in India. The level of poverty was obviously much less because as we had the Welfare State. I am not trying to compare the two. But compared with the family I belonged to, there was truly little that was exceptional about these people. I saw the wealth. I also saw the old and lonely and desperate people. I saw the hand to mouth existence of a weekly wage. I saw the spending habits of poor English people. Friday night was always 'good time' because they had their pay packets. Many were out of money by the following Tuesday.

When I first read 'Lord of the Flies' by William Golding, I could relate to it very much. But even more than the message, it was the simplicity of the language that stayed with me. Learning to listen and learning to speak was what dissolved the barriers between us. With girls it was always easier. Perhaps that is because attraction does not require language.

I was lucky because I was a good looking and health boy. When we arrived in 1965, physically I was as strong as any 11-year-old. We had led an outdoor life, worked with animals, ploughed our fields, ridden on camels and sometimes even horses. In our house we had two dogs. But we did not allow the dogs to lick our faces.

Even while we were being discriminated against, there were things we felt superior about. We also came from a place that discriminated against the lower classes. I came from an 'upper-class' family of landowners. As a child however, I was taught to hold Brahmins is high esteem. They were the learned caste and had a shortest route to Heaven, so I was told. But the Brahmins in my village came to our house to be fed, to be respected. We did not go to their homes. We were owners. We were wealthier comparted to most of our neighbours. We had servants. We gave money to the poor and donated money to the Temple. My father had helped to build the village school. We had our own little gangs in our village. One side against the other. There were family feuds. Land disputes. Teenagers fight everywhere to assert their identities. In our village we were dominant. This changed in England. But if one has occupied a position of dominance, it is almost impossible to become submissive. We were not going to allow white boys to intimidate us. But the white boys were not going to be easily or quickly convinced.

The 1960's were turbulent years. The Vietnam war, the Beatles, Martin Luther King, John Kennedy's assassination among other things such as the Hippy culture and Mohamed Ali. There were so many questions and so much in the air. So much division and yet so much harmony, ambition, and desire for change. Harold Wilson was Prime Minister when we arrive in England in 1965. Even though my English was poor we could sense that England was a progressive nation, looking forward to the future which was becoming increasingly diverse. We wondered why we were here. As children we appeared to be doing perfectly well in the Punjab. Of course, at the age of 11 one does not comprehend the difficulties of life and the ambitions of one's parents. My father had links with England and England opened the door at a time when there was much need for foreign labour.

Harold Wilson with his pipe was impressive and I grew to admire him as I slowly learnt the language and even more slowly became part of the fabric. We were living and experiencing racism all around. Our parents were being denied jobs because my father wore a turban. Indian men and women were often more educated. People who had been Head Teachers back home were working as bus conductors. Engineers worked on the shop floors. There was much debate and discussion about inequality. The fact that we could see conflict between right and wrong made us feel comfortable that change was afoot. People with jobs did not complain. The weekly wages were enough to pay the rent, have food on the table, keep the homes heated and much else, compared to the village we had left behind where for many the yearly monsoon or lack of could result in crops being destroyed or wither because of lack of water. England was safer. Harold Wilson spoke so eloquently and yet I could imagine a man with rotten and stained teeth from the smoking.

From the beginning I have not participated in British politics. The main reason for that, as I now look back, was that as foreigners, we were always the subject of their discussions. We were the pawns the politicians and journalists played with. In the early days it was Enoch Powell and his hate speeches. Enoch Powell was a great orator. In making his arguments I do think that he ever considered that teenage brown and black kids were also part of his audience. The Teddy Boys Enoch Powell so excited went on rampages, and like the characters of 'A Clockwork Orange' victimised innocent foreigners, including one time, my own parents. There were years when I was bitter with rage. If I had a magic wand, I would have made the skinheads and Enoch Powell disappear. I would have turned them into dust.

Exactly who comes out better in a hate struggle is debatable. It depends on the amount of damage caused. Clearly if white people burn a 17-year-old to death, one can argue that they won that battle. But such actions are not an end in themselves. The perpetuators must live with the knowledge of those crimes and those attitudes, which they transmit, like a disease, to their families and friends. They infect and by so doing spoil themselves. And such people, when they are infected, become less than what they could have been.

I personally feel that the winners in life are not the thugs, the racists, and the nationalists. The winners are people who understand that our individual time as living beings is relatively short. The winners are those who understand and appreciate the diversity and the struggles of existence for all in a journey to survive. But the selfish do not look at life that way. They get absorbed by boundaries that language and political systems have perpetuated and want to protect those boundaries as if they were unique and sacred. They lose themselves in themselves and do not appreciate the beauty and harmony with which we are all ultimately connected.

Why did Brexit come about? What are the traits and personal experiences, beliefs, and myths that the English carry with them that makes them think that they are exceptional? Does believing in exceptionalism works to our collective detriment? Great Britain and England are now also mine. There is no getting away from the reality that we have been bound together for centuries and since 1965 I have been part of England as a living, breathing, contributing citizen. I have a stake in our country, and I will not simply watch unreasonable, extremists hijack our future.

Brexit has happened. Brexit does not reflect well on our society. It will cost us. It will diminish our prospects. It need not have happened. Perhaps these pages will suggest that we can have a different future for Great Britain by being better informed, being more vocal and by participating in shaping our common destiny.

Politics of hate

I have been watching the going on in our House of Parliament for 40 years. It is difficult to distinguish often if it is theatre or serious politics. The same party lines are repeated over and over. It amazes me that politicians take themselves seriously. They have been taught by their political advisors to keep their messages simple and to repeat the same messages over and over. On TV one can get to know the behaviour of MPs and the characters they portray. One can get a sense of divisions and one can try to understand the motivations. But it is difficult to comprehend how constituents end up electing their representatives. One cannot understand exactly how a Jacob Rees-Mogg convinces people to vote for him until one looks carefully at the constituency he represents and what type of people live there.

Rees-Mogg was born the year I moved to London. He is the Member of Parliament for North East Somerset. He is estimated to be worth over £200 million. He is extremely religious and is against same sex marriage and abortion. Since he is clearly unable to abstain, the result is that his wife has been subjected to a lot of child births. Given the population of the world is so high, having too many children at this time in human history, is irresponsible. Purely on that observation, a sensible citizenry should not be electing someone like Rees-Mogg as their representative in Parliament. Rees-Mogg is described as a Eurosceptic, but if one listens, one can sense that he hates the EU. He will tell you that he loves his country. He is fond of quoting from old English literature and often uses Latin phrases to illustrate his point and to 'show off' how learned he is. Rees-Mogg campaigned for Leave in the 2016 referendum. He is a member of the European Research Group (ERG), which I can only describe as the 'nationalist' wing of the Conservative Party. In some respects, the ERG is a party within a party. The ERG does not put out any useful research. It certainly is not a think tank. It is a pressure group that receives funding from the Tory government, to push its members political objectives. The use of public funds to push an extremist agenda, or any agenda for that matter, should be a serious concern for our democracy.

Politically I have been relatively inactive all my life. My father came from a country where he saw politics as a dirty and corrupt business. When I was young, around our family table we discussed the Nehru dynasty and the corruption in the Punjab. The bribes one had to pay to get even small tasks accomplished. The connections one needed to get a job as a teacher or a policeman.

In England I didn't join a political party. One brother was a member of the Socialist Party in the 1970's. He brought literature home and I read stuff written by Karl Marx, Lenin, and Trotsky. We followed what was happening in China under Mao. At University I saw how left-wing propaganda was being put together and distributed. I saw how perfectly reasonable people, when they start to adhere to a particular party or a set of values, become blind to alternative realities. As a scientist, I was not impressed by how fluid politics was. I feel that we know the difference between right and wrong, just, and unjust, poverty and wealth, education, and lack thereof. But to change deliberately our own stand and compromise, mislead or misguide, was not something I could readily brush over. At University, my friends and professors told us that those were the usual tools of formulating a political strategy. Adhering to a consistent political message was the only way to define what one stood for and to distinguish oneself from the others, the opposition. I have never seen myself as 'Us and Them.' For me humanity is a single dominion. The weighing up of priorities and allocation of resources for the optimal outcomes of societies should be the objective. Not the frequent swing from socialist to capitalist manifestos.

Early this year, in 2019, I paid for the first time to become member of the Liberal Democrats – a Party I have since observed more closely. After reading their long-term policy agenda I have already decided not to renew my membership. I joined only because I followed Vince Cable for years. The party's pro-

Remain stance was along the lines I agreed with. However, I disagreed with Jo Swinson and her raw and unfounded ambition to be elected as British Prime Minister. The new leader, Ed Davey, may change things for the better, but that is unlikely. Change is not easy for old established parties because of continued reliance on future membership fees and perception that members joined because of what the party stands for, when in fact many join simply to choose the lesser evil.

A political party such as the Liberal Democrats would always be afraid to lose their traditional support. I personally disagree with the Lib Dems on their stance on keeping nuclear weapons. The party has no commitment to free higher education and is relatively indifference to issues of class divisions and racism. Because I was not born in this country, my love for this land and our people happened over decades. As a young man I saw the plight of the poor when I did the newspaper rounds in the Council Estates in Hounslow and Twickenham. I saw it when my mother opened the brown envelope containing the weekly cash my father brought home from British Rail. My love for the vulnerable took hold when I learnt that the rich owned The Sun and The Mail. They fed the contents to the poor. Contents that kept them poor by creating daily rituals that absorbed them - reading gossip, betting on horse races, buying lotto tickets, smoking, and drinking. The least well off in our society are more interested in trivia about what some member of the Royal Family is up to or which porn star has revealed her boobs. The habits that our working classes have formed over generations are what keeps them poor. Their 'interests' their addictions have been conditioned into them by cheap newspapers. They want to be like the celebrities they read about or watch on TV. As a class, they have not learnt how to save. They are in a constant search for the next 'For Sale' item, the Pound Shop, or a free inducement. Most believe that we live in a free society. Capitalism has evolved that way. How free are we when our wages run out before or by the next payday?

I took me time to understand how a newspaper that costs 5p to produce could be distributed for 3p. McDonalds, KFC, Burger King, and the likes of Paddy Power make up the difference and the profits.

In the 1970's I went on demonstrations against the Vietnam War, the Miners, Women's Rights and for Freedom in South Africa and Rhodesia. There were a lot of causes in the 1960s and 1970s. The Cold War was in full swing. The Soviet Union had become the main foreign competitor for political ideology. The Soviet Union put a man into orbit around the Earth, Kennedy embarked America on a mission to the moon. Then, as now, success is often seen through the prism of singular success stories. Average living standards in the Soviet Union were far below American. The competition between the political systems, the resulting Cold War, the fears induced by it, kept the populations silent when governments on both sides spent billions of dollars on weapons of mass destruction or the Space Program. It was all about us and them.

The world was divided then. It remains divided. The old threat of Soviet Union has been replaced by new fears. For the average, The Sun or The Mirror reading citizens, the new threat is still Russia and increasingly China. The West and America are obsessed with China becoming the biggest economy in the world. Everyone is afraid of interference in our elections and politics. We are told that the Cyber Wars are playing increasingly big part in determining election outcomes and stealing of intellectual property. These fears are the drivers of our political positioning. Governments always manipulate their citizens. The most effective tools of mass manipulation are those that create divisions.

In Great Britain, Labour promises higher wages, better education, better NHS, more equality. The Tories come in and promise more national pride, responsible public finances, low corporate taxes. Since the 1970s not much has changed in terms of relative wealth gaps between the rich and the poor. In fact, the wealth gaps have only widened. This is the case in almost all countries. Wealth is becoming concentrated in fewer hands. Relatively Bill Gates has become wealthier compared to how wealthy he was, say 20 years ago. The asset owners in general have taken a bigger and bigger slice of the pie. Putin has become much wealthier in the last 20 years.

The internet gives us access to everything. But what we choose to read, what knowledge we choose to access is limited to who we are and who has influence on our values and behaviour. The working classes still only choose to gamble or accumulate useless inventories. The working classes spend their time watching Chelsea, The Crown, or Love Island, when the well to do go to the theatre or are learning about investing or more efficient ways to increase or collect rent. The poor are safely kept from thinking or complaining as they spend their time in fantasy or reminiscing about a long past era of British greatness. Unfortunately, those glorious days are not coming back.

I do not have political loyalties or consumer product passions. The choices between the Conservatives and Labour Party are stark. They are the opposites. The last Labour government was a centrist party under Tony Blair. While Britain made good progress in the first two terms, the last was spent with Tony Blair paying homage to George W Bush and following him into a deceitful and unnecessary war. That misadventure not only cost hundreds of thousands of lives but triggered other instabilities in the Middle East from which we have yet to recover. Millions of innocent people have been made homeless and turned into refugees. Thousands have drowned while escaping from their former homes and trying to reach the shores of Europe. That wave of immigrants hitting the shores of Europe resulted in new resentments. Invariably described as a 'flood of undocumented migrants.' With many losing their lives at sea, our guilt and hate buttons are pressed at the same time. For the average person, who is already financially stretched, foreigners coming into our country must seem like their own hopes diminished. The cries for immigration controls end up becoming louder. The cries to control our borders become justified. The case for exit from the EU becomes more concrete in these minds. It becomes, once again, about us and them.

The way our democracy has evolved, and this could be a flaw in the democratic model, power has become concentrates in just two parties. We don't seem to have a way to find a new direction or an alternative.

Take Jeremy Corbyn. The Labour Party now has his stamp of approval on it. I agree with a vast number of his positions. Free education, because I received a free education when my parents could not have afforded to pay fees. Cheaper public transport. Again, I wouldn't have been able to afford travel on the Underground and British Rail unless my father's job with British Rail gave us low-cost travel. I am for basic utilities being under Public ownership. One can't pay out dividends to shareholders and still have enough money to invest and keep prices down. It is true that in the 1970's public owned companies acquired a bad reputation. Perhaps they overemployed and were generous with their pension schemes or even tolerated less efficiency. But those are issues to be addressed by government and management. Those are expectations we need to have as a society. The merit of public ownership in certain vital sectors cannot be easily disputed.

But even if I agree with Jeremy on 90% of his agenda, I do not agree with him on the 10%. That 10% may be crucial to my vision of Britain. That vision is a pro-European Britain. Jeremy is complacent about Europe. So, Jeremy doesn't have my vote. I am not a supporter of the Labour Party. I know that many people feel the same way as I do. But because we are fighting for the 10%, we are unable to budge Jeremy. That means that on the most important issue in a generation or two, we are stuck with a leader who is quietly supporting Brexit. Why? Because Jeremy has calculated that the Labour Leave voters are important for him to become Prime Minister – even though the Leave Members of the Labour Party are a small minority.

Secretly, I feel that Jeremy quite likes the idea of Brexit because as politicians the power comes from control of spending decisions. Bringing back the EU contributions we make to Westminster is a salivating dream of any government in power because modern politics is not about what is best for country, it is only about the thirst for personal power and the wish to keep opponents out of power.

This Labour Party also wants to have its cake and eat it. They want to opt out of free movement, thereby being able to control our borders, even though incoming migrants can be made to pay for benefits before they receive a penny.

I can see that the pressures on our NHS or transport builds up if more and more people come to London. We have a booming economy and London is one of the great cities in the world. I can see the pressure on our public services as a valid reason to control or limit the influx. But incoming people bring money and skills that our economy needs. They don't stay unless they find a way to earn. I can buy into the proposition that we need to control the population of our cities and the country. But no one has come up with such policies.

The reality is that we need to add to the numbers, either to simply fill the vacancies or to help us cope with the services we must provide to our own citizens. Britain simply hasn't planned for generations to cultivate enough people with the skills we require to compete in the new economy. The politicians are simply not sharing the hard facts about modern Britain and its place in the European and global ecosystem.

We have a choice as a nation. We can scale down our ambitions to be a leading economy in the world. We can choose to make Britain a truly sustainable country. No net increase in our population, lower growth that takes account of the environment and human happiness perhaps. If we had such a vision, then perhaps we can sell an isolationist agenda. But that also is not what is confronting us. That is not reality. The reality is that the whole planet is in a state of flux. Climate change being one important driver. But without Climate Change there are many other dynamics at play. Populations are on the move for complex reasons. Growth in the Emerging Markets is its own driver of change. Growth means that Britain can avail itself of the investment opportunities. Opportunities are not one-way streets. It requires collaborations and movements of good and services and thus people. We shut our doors to foreigners, we are shutting ourselves in. The emerging foreigners will also not permit us into their homes with open arms. And that can only lead to our decline as a nation.

We have an ageing population. We need foreigners to look after them!

The history of nations is not the history of a race or the colour of people's skins or preservations of some tenuous values, culture, traditions, or religion. A great history is made of influx and exodus, of movement and migration or intermarriage and cross culture exchange of love and hopes. The United States didn't come into its present state because people refused to move. It was murderous and bloody. It wasn't about closing doors. It wasn't about not embracing reality and shaping it.

There are about 10% of the Tory policies I agree with. For the most part the Tory Party doesn't deserve to be in power.

When people buy The Sun to check out the betting pages., inadvertently they ended up reading the political messages and inevitably with frequent readings of the same hate embedded biases they become the characters they are. They end up believing the lies told and the divisions caused by the owners of The Sun. I don't understood why in Britain the working classes vote for the Tories. The Tory message is always about patriotism and deferred promises. Every election cycle, immigration is revived and revved up as an issue. Anti-EU sentiment comes to the fore. New promises are made and never kept. Deferred promises for people who are struggling and see no way out is as good as belief in God.

Similarly, the Left, while overall promotes social justice and greater equality gets entrenched in one or two extreme policies which end up dividing the have and have nots. Most haves are reasonably willing to create a more just society, but rebel when asked to go the extra mile. They have seen the experiments with socialism elsewhere and concluded that it doesn't work. Everyone overlooks the progress of China. Instead, we refocus on what Britain did with its own socialist experiments. That conjures up images of strife and divisions.

My personal view is that for Socialism to take root in a democracy it needs time that is far longer than the 5-year election cycle. Genuine Socialism takes time to implement and implementation is never smooth. We are a society that wants instant gratification even when our problems are entrenched and have rigidified over the long term. We are not interested in social progress on a massive scale, as in China, where more people have been lifted out of poverty in the last 50 years than at any other time in human history. The conservatives want individual freedoms to prosper in a 'dog eat dog' world. Socialism is about social change. Conservatism is more about individual dominance. The Conservatives will forever remember the miners' strike and the Trade Union movement as destructive forces. The Trade Unions were slayed by Margaret Thatcher, our so-called Iron Lady. Conservatives, by definition, don't want social progress.

On either side of The Right and The Left we have the extremists. If I had to choose between an extremist who is on the far Left or on the far Right, I would always choose the far Left. The Right is usually unfair, and the extreme Right is downright dangerous. The maximum damage one can cause on the far Left is give away some freebees to perhaps some underserving people. On the far Right, they hang people or enslave them.

Not that the far left hasn't left a history littered with corpses. The revolutions in Russia and China left millions of dead and homeless. Perhaps the surrender of power from the far-Right is only possible through bloody revolutions. Peaceful transitions to democracy are rare. This is not the place to argue if those revolutions were justified.

What is democracy in any case? If the system is corrupted by the lure or bait of winning millions or free vouchers for your next outing, then what is democracy? If we live in a social framework where education is denied or is sub-par for the majority then what is democracy? To be able to vote is a great privilege. But to vote in ignorance of the impact of outcomes or as Trump may call it Fake News, then what is democracy? Of course, in the case of Trump it is 'a pot calling a kettle black'. He is a fake president and is a far-Right extremist, who would hang innocent people or build a wall to stay in and keep them out.

Human history is in many respects quite short. For the most part we have been a primitive tribal bunch. Driven by scarcity in the natural environment we have a desire to group for defensive purposes, accumulate and have natural opposition to sharing. Darwin will have it that all species promote the survival of the fittest. With humanity, survival starts with the individual, extends to family, then to community and possibly then to the species. Our primitive instincts are to attack anything that we consider different. The greater the difference the easier we find to make enemies. Family first, then cousins, then own tribe and then other tribes that look the same and so on and so on. That explains why the white man has inflicted the worse kinds of savageries on the blacks. They turned Africans into slaves and Indian into lackeys. I am not saying for one moment that had history turned out to be different, the Black people would not have turned Whites into slaves and Indians into lackeys. Primitive is embedded into our genetic code. Instincts do serve an extremely useful purpose in perhaps avoiding imminent danger, but instincts are on the whole inferior to intellect and being able to reason. Instincts don't project consequences.

History shows us that intellect doesn't necessarily translate to knowledge and knowledge doesn't always translate to wisdom.

Perhaps humanities biggest failing has been to believe that the natural order is the right order. It isn't. Nazi Germany was promoted on Darwinian philosophy. Nature itself, we know, is the result of accidental environmental conditions and random selection to adopt to it. Nature is not the intelligent choice. Nature is merely a choice that tries to survive the best it can in a given eco system.

Politics often defines and fixes us in some place imagined by others. Karl Marx thought and wrote about the rise of capitalism and its inevitable ultimate collapse. Prolifically Karl Marx defined the Socialist Space, which has been followed by millions of people to define themselves. The ultimate collapse may take generations or may never happen. In the meantime, humanity makes progress and changes at many if not all levels. Political theory on the other hand can remain stagnant for very much longer and becomes unsuitable to run society. The basic tenants ought not change. Fair income distribution, equal opportunity, need for health care in wealthy societies, decent education, equality for minorities and genders, protecting our environment etc. ought to remain lasting values. But they don't because in functioning democracies self-interest starts to assert itself and degrades common interest. Not only that. Truth and values are no longer absolute. Genetic engineering and manipulations, AI, big data, VR is changing everything, including the meaning of life and what it is to be alive.

I am the product of our politics. I have been fighting racism since the age of 11. At some point in my late twenties, I decided that I wasn't interested in making a case for it. I decided that my world can do well without anyone who showed racist behaviour. It wasn't important for me to know them or interact with them. For years I chose to simply avoid them, and in my mind said to myself that, 'they don't need to be part of my life.' It is not that I would tolerate being discriminated against. But then what can one do if the system operates along bias lines? What can one do if one is turned down for jobs simply because the colour of one's skin? How should one react? Protest? Fight? Expose? All that takes time and money. On the other hand, a person with confidence can make another life and forget about the racist. It may be a less lucrative life. But it is genuine and dignified.

As I reflect now, I had the seeds of anti-racism in me even before I was 11-years old. In our village we had the untouchables and low caste. When we gave them bread, we threw it into their stretched hands. I remember looking into the beautiful eyes of an un-scrubbed child still as I was told not to touch them. My natural desire or instinct as a child was to pick them up. I remember losing something in myself as I obeyed my elders. Alas, I digress. But these memories are important in giving insights into how I have evolved and finally chose to be a British Citizen. I use capital 'C' in my form of citizenship because I wasn't born with a British identity. I acquired it in my late teens by choice. My father kept his Indian passport for years longer because it was so hard for him to shed his old skin, whereas I had by then interacted enough, read enough, seen enough to know that Britain was a more progressive nation. I had witnessed Enoch Powell and the responses to his kind of Britain. Already by the time of The Race Relations Act of 1968, I was conscious that the British government was making it illegal to discriminate against people like myself. That we were being given equal rights. Of course, looking back now, unless one puts it in historical perspective, to a teenager it wasn't apparent that racism should even exist, because we were opposing in our classrooms and in the playground any attempt to discriminate by the white boys. We didn't see them as superior or special.

When I worked at Deutsche Bank in the 1980's it was a very much German institution. The senior people in the twin towers in Frankfurt didn't trust the English any more than the English trusted the Germans. As a brown man one can imagine I could not easily entertain the idea of very many Germans reporting to me. There was a natural glass ceiling. Still, I managed to make some German friends. Perhaps it was because I was not English that they in time, opened to me. Most Germans I found to be decent, well educated, practical and tolerant. But there were others who 30 years after WWII were still reciting Jewish jokes. The jokes were ghastly. 30-years after WWII one could still detect evil in German society. Now more than 70-years after WWII we have the AltRight. German democracy tolerates it. The German people live with it because we still haven't worked out what 'Democracy' means. We haven't worked out the difference between right and wrong. We haven't worked out the difference between being a human being and defining oneself as a nationalist. This is the pace at which humanity progresses.

During those years at Deutsche Bank, I also discovered a lot of positive aspects to Germany. The country was not divided along Class lines as in the United Kingdom. Most Germans were better dressed, more travelled, better informed. There appeared to be much less inequality among them. They worked hard. German companies were more efficient, the German workers more skilled. The Germans I met, were also less engaged in the world politics. They were becoming increasing more engaged through their industry, but when it came to geopolitics the Germans appeared not to have views. It was as if they were afraid to be engaged. Afraid to say anything that might bring about a retort of some sort to reflect their past. Most Germans were repentant about their Nazi past and subdued by it. Their answer seemed to be to volunteer no answers, to not engage. Despite that, they were patriotic. They wanted to see a strong Germany. Industrial prowess was their answer to having been defeated in WWII. They wanted to show the English that they will end up having a better nation rising out of the rubble. They were working to have higher average living standards compared to Britain and America.

In the 19080's Deutsche Bank was a stable institution and extremely powerful. The bank basked in self-confidence. The Bank had large holding in major German industrial groups such a Bayer and Daimler. There was a great Art Collection. The top floors at Leadenhall Street were covered wall to wall with original works. We were treated to some of the best German wines when we invited guests for lunch.

When I visited Frankfurt, I noticed that the streets were cleaner compared with London. I noticed too that, overall, German food was better. German beer was much better.

My actual experience of Germany and the Germans was quite contrary to the message that had been drilled into me at school in London and my University years. The English boys hated the Germans. Dad's Army was their key reference point together with war documentaries and war movies. Even though we had won, after WWII, as victors, we didn't forgive. The Germans, I felt, hadn't forgiven themselves for the crimes of their fathers. The young Germans wanted to move on and build bridges in Europe.

What we saw was a Germany that was renewing itself and once again slowly but surely surpassing us once again. That was a source of resentment and envy. We weren't reflecting how we might do better and compete with the onslaught of the losers of WWII – the Japanese and the Germans. We continued to perpetuate a divisive class structure which gave advantage to primarily the top few percent of the population. In contrast, German free education was becoming the envy of Europe. Now that Germany has become the largest economy in Europe and left us in the limelight our bitterness is even greater. And how do we respond as a nation? We vote for Brexit. We are not willing to be at the same table where the country we defeated in two wars dares to exercise more influence on European policy – even when they contribute significantly more to the EU's budget!

We never cared very much about the French, Italians or the Spanish. We drink their wine and enjoy their food and go to those destinations for holidays or for second homes. But when we go there most of us don't talk to them, we don't speak their language. We go and congregate among English speaking people.

Our ability to mix with the Europeans is far less compared with their ability to mix with us. They understand our jokes. They have seen Monty Python, Morecombe and Wise, Faulty Towers and Mr. Beans. While this is a tribute to our creative arts, which of their comedians do we admire? What jokes have we learned to share with them?

For a people that had ruled the world the English are extremely insular. I remember when we arrived in England and moved into our first house. We were the only Indian family on the street. Our white neighbours didn't reach out to us for years. I played with white kids at school, but never with our neighbours. The only people who came to our door were the Christians from the church on our street or Jehovah's Witnesses.

We spoke with the Christians and convinced them that in many ways our faith was similar. Like them, we believed in One God, the father of Jesus Christ. They believed in life after death and as did we. Sikh's perhaps believed more in this life. With Jehovah's Witnesses, we had absolutely nothing in common. We told them to leave their literature and promised to read it. I read some of the stuff they left behind. It had little impact. It all ended up as fodder to feed our coal fires.

Our neighbours were not racists. Because they didn't talk to us, we assumed they were at the time. In the years to come, their daughter turned out to be quite beautiful and was attracted to one of my brothers. We communicated more as we grew older. And what did we discover? That they too lived rather simply. They kept their curtains drawn so that passers-by in the street couldn't peep in. The husband and wife sat in their living room, read books and smoked a lot. When we saw that their house was modestly furnished and smelled of cigarettes, we were quite happy not to be playing with their kids all those years. My parents would not have permitted it. We had our own snobberies.

English parents encouraged their kids to go out to work and for them to have relationships at relatively early age. Many working-class parents have children and then can't wait for the day when they will move out. Economic insecurity may have a lot to do with it. Most people when they have children don't calculate the cost of raising them. In the days when the vast majority were employed in factories, seeing them leave home and take up jobs must have seemed like a good solution. The world has changed. Skills and knowledge are what distinguishes one potential employee from the next.

Our relative advantages as a nation have been withered away by our attitudes towards our own people. We worked them in factories for generations and paid them only a minimum living wage. We kept them in their place by promoting trivial media and encouraged addictive interests such as Horse Racing or supporting football teams. We had them waving flags and worshipping David Beckham. What are they left with as they get older? How much of their earnings have they flittered away in booze, gambling, and football games in proportion to what they spent on their children and planning a secure future?

As relatively poor immigrants, we were different. Education was the primary goal of the family. Some form of family unity and an attitude to take care of each other was a running theme. The average house price in 1967 for a 5-bedroom house in Isleworth was say £5000. The weekly wage for my father may have been £30. The average house price in the UK may well have been 4-5 times the average annual salary. But within 4 years of my father arriving in the UK, we were proud homeowners. How did we do it? By putting our savings into the same pot. By saving money month by month and by borrowing from close relatives any short fall. Even with just a few friends or relatives around, we helped each other. My parents made the sacrifices because for them there was no greater reward than to see their children flourish. They had suffered from shortages during WWII and after India's independence. They had been frustrated by the lack of opportunities in India with its bureaucracy and corruption. England gave them the opportunity to work and save perhaps for the first time in their lives. They embraced it. As we worked and saved and established our roots our confidence grew. We weren't wearing the same pair of trousers for months on end as in the earlier days. House prices started to go up. In 10 years, the house that we brought for £5000 was worth £30,000. And in ten years the youngest among us had completed his degree in Pharmacy from Liverpool Polytechnic. We were on our way to full integration because now my brother was responsible in some measure for the health of the community.

I digress. The reason is that I want to explain how one becomes who one is. The 11-year old Punjabi boy who one day was out in the fields with his herd of cows and next day on a BOAC plane headed first to Moscow and then Heathrow and then brought to Ealing in a Black Cab and subjected to a completely new set of conditions doesn't and cannot remain anchored to his culture or his country of birth. That 11-year-old adapts and tries to understand the new world, the new people and their culture and superstitions. After many years of learning, arguing, fighting, understanding, fearing, forgiving, losing, and winning one hopes that the product that survives and cherishes the new home has claimed it also as his own. Claimed it to an extent to say that this England, this Great Britain is also mine. In the process of that transformation of the self, one has in some small but significant way also transformed the new home and its occupants. I am part of the British reality.

Your England is my England. Your Britain is my Britain. Your Britain is not the same as it was or same as how it might have been without my presence. I have made you pregnant and I am also your child. I am your product and part of your imagination. Deal with it.

What is it that I cherish about Britain? Obviously, there are many things that one falls in love with. I personally don't admire Britain because of its Empire. I have every reason to resent that period of history when the Indian were so weak or disorganised and, in many ways, backward that they (we) didn't care who ruled over us. The price they paid was to be governed by the British for 200 years. We can't know to what extent that stunted the natural growth of India. We can't know if industrialisation would have taken root or if India would have broken up into many states and subcultures. Since we can't know, let us not focus on what could have been.

Without Empire, perhaps I would not have been born. But what happened was of equal significance for our lives. Britain ended up having an influence. Some links were created. Many stories were told. Much progress was made. Many atrocities were committed. Bonds were formed and broken. Literature was shared. The imagination of Kipling was lit up. Landscapes and architecture were changed. Dependencies were created. Indian soldiers were called to fight in WWI and WWII. India made a difference to the future of Great Britain. We were linked through the stories and the shedding of our grandparents' blood for the causes of Great Britain and our own cause, our own destiny was linked to that. Thus, the cause of Great Britain and Europe for that matter, became our cause.

Had we not won the two great wars, who knows what would have become of India? I dread to think of an India under Hitler. But then again, undisturbed, India may very well have given birth to a Nazi like country. Fixed ideologies, firm beliefs, and romantic adherence to a long lost perceived or even a real great past leads to no good. People need to be guided by current reality. Current knowledge about the nature of reality, creation, and physics. Allowing religion to shape our destiny is primitive.

Beyond those links of the contributions our forefathers made to the survival of Great Britain, there were other things to love. As a teenager as I started to study science, I was in awe of the great many British scientists who brought about the scientific revolution. From Isaac Newton, James Maxwell, Charles Darwin, Michael Faraday, Ernest Rutherford to Steven Hawking, our history is rich in the field of discovery. If one starts to understand and appreciate the contributions of Great Britain and Europe to humanities progress one can't then not want to associate with it. Who doesn't want to belong to a tradition of learning?

Everyone speaks of Shakespeare. I am not going to. Beyond Shakespeare, Britain has produced great writers. And we have shared them with the world so that the world associates with us as a people. Our literature hides nothing and tells it as it was as best as it could. I do not see conspires when I read Kipling. I just see a man who observed life from his viewpoint. It was his reality or fiction. Most of all it was a good story, even though even good stories can distort our view of the world. Our literate depicts what it is that we are still struggling with today – a society divided along class or wealth. Greater equality in Great Britain remains a long- term project in 2018. Of course, we have progressed immensely from the time of Charles Dickens. But poverty has not been eradicated. Neither has the blight of Class.

It is not just sciences and literature. The Europeans produced the most amazing musicians. Britain promoted that music and made it its own. Slowly, I started to appreciate Mozart more than the Sitar, the Beatles more than Mohamed Rafi. If I were a vessel that could only be filled with different aspects of culture, I was shedding some or diluting my Indian part and replacing it with what I admired about Great Britain. But where would Great Britain be without Europe?

When Britain had its Empire so did the Europeans. If one visits Spain, Austria, France, Belgium, Portugal, Holland one can see how much wealth they brought back and how rich they became through those dominations. One can see it in their buildings and museums and art collections. If one looks at how much scientific overlap there has been in Europe, then one cannot say that we could have done it on our own. We would not have won the 2nd World War without Albert Einstein or Neil Bohr. If we couldn't have done it on our own for the last 300 years, why are we withdrawing now? Do we want to be separate from Europe in mind and spirit even? Why are we divorcing?

We are divorcing because we have illusions about ourselves as individuals and as a people. We have been drip-fed about how great we were. Except for a few percent of the Great British population that benefited from the Great British Empire, most just suffered it. When Gandhi came to Britain before independence, he visited the cotton mills in the Midlands. Those workers were employed under atrocious conditions. They and millions like them didn't benefit, except perhaps in a trickle-down way, from the riches of the Empire. It was only the Trade Union Movement in the 1960 that started to make progress on workers' rights and better pay. But all those people in the Midlands who voted for Brexit still think that they can be 'great' again. They are the very people who have been neglected by Westminster and wealthy England. We haven't invested in them for the last 50 years. As soon as the Iron foundries, coal mines, tin mines, and cotton mills and finally the car manufacturing plants were gone, we did nothing to revive the Midlands. Most the money went to London and the rich South West. Go to Liverpool, Derby, Coventry, Leicester and look for yourself. Great Britain through these lenses is under stress and poor in comparison to reginal cities in Germany, France, Canada, Australia, Austria etc.

Where does this unfounded pride come from? Is it a form of survival instinct? The French have a national desire to differentiate themselves from the English? Poor people in India who have nothing, take pride in the fact that they can do without. But pride can be extremely self-defeating. It is the story of a boy who stays away from school because all the other kids are better dressed.

If one is poor, the only way out of the trap is through better education. I am not blaming the poor people from the Midlands. I am married to a girl whose family came from Derby. I have walked the streets and talked with the locals. From my own relatively poor background I sympathise with them and always feel like hugging them. But such is the condition in which we have locked them up. Unable to move to even London, let alone Barcelona, Frankfurt, or Paris. Unable to afford any type of move because they have no savings.

For millions of citizens in our United Kingdom, it is a hand to mouth existence. Even in Hounslow, young people working in shops earn say £350 per week. They pay around £125 on rent. Utility bills, telephone, transport ends up say £50. They go out once a week and spend £20. The girls, when they go to the hairdressers, end up spending £40. Food £100? It doesn't leave very much for a holiday or emergency. They cannot afford to have a Costa Coffee every day!

We pride ourselves as being the 5th largest economy on the planet. But the lives of the many revolve around eating junk food, watching reality shows, and spending more money on our nails than we do on reading books. I know of no other nation that is so rich and yet still so poor. We need to wake up as a people and look at what we do each day and how we consume our time and energy. The people in charge need to wake up and look at the world we are living in. The Italians, Spanish, are catching up and much of Northern Europe, France, Switzerland, Germany are all ahead of us. Brexit will further reduce both the prospects for the UK and the outlook for the future.

We must stop hating the people around us. We need to strive for greater empathy and think of our lives and theirs as fragile. Many of us are just passing through as best as we can.

One loses nothing through collaboration. There is much to gain. My politics is pro-European.

The roots of English Brexit

Once upon a time there was the British Empire!

Except that it wasn't British at all. It was the English Empire, and for a long time before it was the East India Company Empire. The English alone dominated the colonies and thereby defined themselves and tried and often succeeded in putting their stamp on those countries. All the colonised were economically backward lands. For many the idea of nationhood or a system of government catering to the needs of all had not evolved. For the most part, the English created or expanded upon the governing institutions and local laws.

The foreign conquests lit the imagination of all English people. The actual colonizers formed views about themselves and the greatness of the English Empire became the national anthem. 'God Save the King or Queen' for everyone to rally behind. It became their reality. The heroes of the English Empire became the ideals of the English nation. England has since been defined by its folklore.

The question is what becomes of a people who come to define themselves in certain rigid ways based on history? Right or wrong the English formed a fixed image of themselves as a people during those 200 odd years of colonial rule. They saw themselves, obviously, as 'the people in charge.' They saw themselves as the civilising force. They saw themselves as more advanced, more just, better educated, more accomplished, more sophisticated, stronger, wiser and heaven forbid meaner. Their ladies rode horses in special impractical positions and wore big hats and corsets and used make up and dangled their hair in waves. The men smoked pipe, dressed in uniforms with swords on the side and big leather boots and grew moustache and played cricket. In time these and other images of what it is to be English got fixed in the national psyche. 'We are the greatest nation on earth', 'We are the rulers', 'We know what is right', 'We are in control', 'We know how to set the rules of governance', 'You will do as we say.' Etc. Etc.

Of course, reality is perceived to be the way we convey it. An English chap with the title of Sargent Major is only going to write letters to his family depicting his authority and his power. He may also depict that he has a nice bungalow and servants and the fact that he enjoys his life in parties with others. He doesn't share how he feels inside when on a horse and in a local setting where he could be pulled down and hacked to death. He doesn't tell his friends ones that he is not free to get to know and make friends with the locals. He doesn't convey his loneliness. Back home though they see only the uniform and the smile and the horse and the big house and they associate that with power and as part of being English. Not that the Sargent didn't visit the local brothels or had concubines or wasn't attracted to boys and didn't experiment with getting high. One can assume and one knows from the resulting changes in complexion of the population and the money transfers that the exploitations of the English unfolded many a sari.

It doesn't matter how wretched your condition may have been in Yorkshire or Sunderland, the Empire instilled a certain sense of pride in the minds of most English people. I don't know if this is true for English women as well to the same extent, but Englishmen associate themselves with these romantic mindsets of 'once upon a time greatness' and the wish for it to be true now.

And then World War II happened. England had drained its resources. Suddenly we had to ask for help from the Americans and rely on our Empire to feed the war spending. America helped us not only to win the war, but then rescued us from economic collapse. But more importantly it was America that shaped the post WWII order. It was America that allowed for and aided the rebuilding of Germany and Japan and depleted us of all the power we had before the war.

Drained of our economic might and having no more will to fight new wars, for surely in the absence or possibly even the continued presence of Gandhi, civil unrest on a scale that Britain could not possibly contain was lurking under the surface and we knew it. The Crown in the Jewel was lost.

More than any other European colonial power, the English are defined by their experiences of the Empire. It was not the conditions of the working classes in the cotton mills of Sheffield that gave them their illusions of grandeur, it was the Queen visiting the, what are now the Commonwealth countries, that shaped their identity.

Of course, there is no such thing as the English. There are the English aristocrats who own the wealth of the nation and have done so for centuries. There are the officers and gentlemen from these classes who commanded the battalions and who often also were sacrificed to maintain the Empire together with underlings who simply obeyed orders. The downtrodden, because their conditions were so insecure, they defined themselves with the projected imagery of the ruling classes. The shopkeepers, the factory floor workers inhabit England, but they have never had a meaningful say in how the country is run. The great transformations happened because there was wealth creation and a new awareness after WWII. Workers fought hard to win some basic rights. The National Health Service (NHS) which is perhaps the greatest civilizing achievement of modern British society was created. Women demonstrated for equality. Education became universal and free. Human rights improved after centuries of slavery and abuse at home. If there is anything tangible by which one can define the unity of purpose it is these social achievements.

But this reconstruction was happening across Europe. It wasn't unique to Great Britain. Across the channel, America was going through its own change, industrial, and Civil Rights. Japan was rebuilding franticly.

Still, England maybe an island within an island, but its scientists and explorers influenced change all over the world. The rest, stay at home kind, were impacted by that change. They imagined with them and were defined by those great people, even though the realities of their personal lives were unaffected by the Empire and those discoveries in the arts and science. Ask any Hindu in the streets of Mumbai. They link themselves to their Gods through those threads of history real or imagined which inspires greatness in themselves. So, it is with the English. To want to hold on to that thread when one has truly little to show for oneself is what defines 'national identity.'

Reconstruction of Britain took decades. During this time, social change was forced and in time Britain relinquished control over all of what was Empire. This happened over a relatively short period of time. As we were giving up control, we were still engaged in a diminishing way in at least influencing the shape of independence. But the English left the colonies in a hurry and without consideration for the wellbeing of the native populations. Bloodshed in India, chaos in Africa that took decades of conflicts and decades to unwind. This abandonment too absorbed us. And then the EU started to form like a growing foetus. Alive, uncontrollable like a force of nature.

In the whirlwind of change, as Japan rose from the wreckage of WWII and Germany rebuilt from the ashes and as America became preoccupied by Vietnam and as we engaged in what post WWII order would look like and as EU took shape and as immigrants from the Commonwealth countries slipped into our country, even though they were invited to rebuild or work the factories, before we could reassess or control, our reality shifted from pre-war to something different. Never mind that this change to globalisation was a direct result of industrialisation and had its origins probably when Mr. Ford put together the assembly line to mass produce cars, the change that took place in Britain didn't allow the English time to evolve their mindset from colonial to post-colonial, post EU, post global. The story of the 'good old days' was still being told by the fireside and somehow many English people expected the world order to revert to the time when they were on top. Perhaps the war had united the English like no nation had been united before, that they saw themselves as one. The spirit of nationalism had been lit, while the flame of internationalism was being extinguished.

England went through a 50-year period of arrested growth, where they were being delinked from the Empire and had to concentrate on survival and having no time to think about the future. The English still have not found what they consider their rightful place in Europe and indeed in the world is. The Germans have figured this out. It is to be an industrial powerhouse, to remain relatively humble and to foremost work towards sustainable economic stability. The world of trading as centred around the City of London just doesn't offer that kind of stability as it is influenced by the winds of change that could originate in Argentina as well as Zimbabwe. We are prune to a hedge fund blowing up in Connecticut or Nigel Lawson taking Sterling out of the European Rate Mechanism. France has always known its place. For whatever reason, the French appear to have a stronger identity. The country is bigger, and the landscape is more varied. Perhaps the French were in fewer and smaller countries. It is possible that India has changed the English a lot more compared to the Algerians having the same influence on the French. Perhaps it is because some of our myths in England were created in India. Or perhaps it is as simple as curry and pints of Cobra.

Whatever the causes instinctively we feel that we belong at the head table in global affairs. Even the Falklands victory has gone to our head. Waging a war in the Middle East shows that we have the soldiers and fighter jets to annihilate poor nations, possibly even subjugate them. We can wage wars and broker peace. We haven't reconciled to the reality that we are much less significant to force change or order in the world. We have been resisting coming to terms with who we now are and what we are capable of and we watch helplessly as our formal colonies have learnt to live without us and in the case of India are growing rapidly and at least in overall economic might are well on their way to supersede us. None look to Great Britain for advice or for solving problems and few expect us to invest in their countries or transfer technology. We have been shrinking from the world stage and this has been palpable to the English. Our response to our declining importance appears to be become even more recluse as if we don't want to play the game anymore.

It is German progress that seems to irritate the English the most. The victors of WWII have stood by as German engineering overtook Britain in manufacturing to become the biggest exporter in the world. They have seen how West Germany wore the costs of the peaceful reunification and West and East Germany to become the biggest economy in Europe. They have seen how the Bundesbank and German politicians have delivered for their people and for Europe and have become more and more influential. Our people drive BMWs and Mercedes and Audi's and think and know that these are status symbols and quality products. The success of Germany irks them. The Scandinavian countries are smaller in economic size, but they too have leapt ahead, with average earnings and living standards much higher compared to England. The English see the French as more cultured. To say nothing of the Dutch, Austrians, even the Italians enjoy living standards that are higher than what we might find in the Midlands. To put simply, the English feel that they are being left behind.

Taking orders as they describe it from Brussels or abiding by the laws of the European Court of Justice and being asked to contribute to common EU budgets and having open borders for EU citizens is not how it was supposed to be. Within the EU, Great Britain of course exerts its influence and shapes common EU policies. But the English don't see it that way. They always want to opt out and have special arrangements. For the most part the EU has granted special arrangement to the UK.

Brexit is the result of being denied more and more opt outs for English exceptionalism.

David Cameron, for all the wrong reasons went forward with a referendum. He hoped the British people will surely vote to Remain. But they voted to Leave. They voted to leave because the Leave campaign packaged the choice in the nations more cherished clothing, the survival of the NHS, and the our nations' worst anxiety, in not wanting more foreigners in the country. Except that the fears of not wanting more foreigners was a relic of colonial past, in not wanting more brown and black people in the country. 'How can they be allowed to come here and then become our equals?' One can also hear the English whispering through gritted teeth – 'We are a special nation. We are a special people.'

It now transpires that the referendum itself was rigged. Cambridge Analytica used clever algorithms to download user data from Facebook. The analysis showed which users could be persuaded by targeted e-mails to vote for Brexit. Now there is more evidence that perhaps Russia intervened in the Brexit process by setting up thousands of accounts and posting pro-Brexit content. It wasn't just that David Cameron's binary choice of a YES or NO vote was absurd and without calculation or planning, the whole issue of Brexit got distilled about one issue and that of immigration. Suddenly one saw the flags of St George being waived by adults and children. England needed to define itself. And that definition was that we are not Europeans. It is unfortunate that we happen to be geographically located in this part of the globe. We were always global, colonizers, and traders and we want to have our freedom to be able to trade across the globe and negotiate our own trading partnerships, which EU membership doesn't allow.

There were other rumblings about the fact that the world outside of the EU is growing at a much faster pace compared with the EU itself and therefore we are going to be doing the right thing. This statement is in fact true and false at the same time. Emerging economies are growing at a faster clip. But the overall size of those economies is still relatively ridiculously small. It may take 50 years for that trade to grow to the size of trade we have with the EU. The absolute absurdity of politicians packaging sound bites in order to divert attention of the unquestioning minds leaves one wordless. Once on a slippery road one cannot know where one will land.

During the whole Brexit vote preparation period the US election campaigning was in progress. Donald Trump was that campaigns most aggressive candidate. His whole approach to politics is based on fake and turning the conventional wisdom upside down. He talked about building a Wall along the whole of the Mexican border. He classified all Mexicans, Muslims and other foreigners as criminals or terrorists and even rapists. This white man's obsession that someone of another colour is sleeping with white women hasn't died. The Brexiters watched Trump and copied the strategy for the UK. Foreigners got associated with terrorism and rape. Foreigners were associated with the crisis in the NHS. Sometimes it was the Romanians and at other times it was the Poles. The average Joe didn't think that white immigrants as a problem when Nigel Farage talked about too many foreigners. They saw who was in their field of vision who was also different. They saw skins of different complexions. Even in the hospitals they didn't focus on the complexion of the patients. They saw the people who were treating them. They saw black, Indian and Pakistani nurses, doctors, cleaners and rubbish collectors. Suddenly they were asking why we have so many of them?

Brexit was not meant to be about ethnic minorities in the UK. Brexit was meant to be about Great Britain leaving the institution called the EU and all that entailed. The sizable number of British voters, predominately English voters voted to Leave because it implied fewer immigrants and possibly that 'taking back control' meant we could also deport the ones who were already here. It was the Paki haters who voted for Brexit just as much as those who can't stand the French and still hate the Germans – except of course when they bring jobs to their locality, in which case they would happily go and work in their factories. In the same way I don't understand how the working classes vote for the Conservatives, I don't understand how they are happy to go and work in a Jaguar assembly plant, go home and shower and eat in an Indian or Pakistani restaurant and do this day in day out and then vote for Brexit!

And the timing turned out to be simply perfect for the vote. Since the financial crisis, inequality in Britain has risen. Wages for the lower paid and the middle classes have been stagnant. Austerity has made the poor more insecure as social programs were curtailed as the funds were diverted to save the banks. The refugee crisis told stories of people drowning at sea and Britain being asked to accept their share. Free Movement suddenly became an unacceptable. Most British households don't have much in savings. About one third of workers in the UK have less than £500 in savings. It is a hand to mouth Britain we live in. Being asked to help those in need at a time of personal insecurity was the cause of retrenchment.

This all shows just how fragile the world we live in is. Goodwill only lasts if everything is going well. In times of scarcity, we turn on our neighbours. In times of nationalism, we go for ethnic cleansing as a tribal response. Just underneath the surface of purported decency, fairness, justice is the primitive instinct.

English racism

Racism is a human evolutionary trait. Humanity evolved as tribes. The homo sapiens tribes wiped out the Neanderthals. Slavery was prevalent in ancient India, in Roman times. The Portuguese started kidnapping people from West Africa in the 15th century. The British and Americans turned slavery into an asset gathering exercise on an industrial scale in the 16th century.

Racial discrimination and racial inequity persist today. Institutionalised racism exists to differing degrees in most countries. The civilizing of humanity has a way to go.

We must face it. Like many others, we are a racist nation. The English are more racist compared with the Scots, the Irish and Welsh people. The English are more racist compared to the Germans, Scandinavians, Dutch, Portuguese, Spaniards, Swiss, and possibly the French and on par with the Italians. This is an obvious and glaring truth about the English. The power of these Isles has resided in London for centuries. England is bigger and thus disproportionately more influential. Probably we have been racist for many generations, well before the Slave Trade. Our arrogance relates to our success and rooted in the Empire itself. It may very well be rooted in Darwinism. The primitive notion that what is true for species should also apply to humanity. Human history is only a history of wars and empire building - one people against another, one nation against another. When we started to discover the laws of nature, we wanted to exploit them first for our people. Discoveries make us relatively more powerful and with power come arrogance. We think of Hitler wanting to create a race of superior humans, perhaps the English wanted to conquer the world and turn it English white. At the start of these overseas conquests, we know there was much slaughter and mayhem. One only has to look at the fate of native Indians and the Aborigines to know the brutality of conquest. But the idea must have taken form at some point that getting rid of them was patriotic or even a divine right. Would it have happened without Darwinism? Of course! The history of conquest goes back to well before Roman times. The Bhagavat Gita depicts great wars and domination over others long before. The British dominance was the latest. It may not be the last. Technology may make for a different type of domination altogether, based on enhanced human beings or super intelligent genes. America is the new global superpower with China not far behind. The new domination is not just military. It is economic and is accomplished through both technology and investment in physical and financial infrastructure.

Yes, to give credit, Britain has also been a civilising force. Linked to our own wealth creation was the need to tame, teach and impart skills to the locals. We had enough practice at exploitation of our underclasses. Perhaps all nations must go through these phases when organising the masses in the process of urbanisation. Capital accumulation has always been at the expense of labour exploitation. Human beings are prolific breeders and until industrialisation genuinely took hold there was never a shortage of workers. There were in human history always more need and want and mouths to feed compared with supply of food and materials. Only now in the developed world we are reaching the point of equilibrium in demand/supply and possibly in a position to create excess supply leading to perpetual or at least very long-term low inflation. Bit modern wealth or economy has gone beyond material abundance. We invent something new, like the internet, and have people pay for simply being connected. Connectivity and all that entails is the new wealth. And all of this is continuing to lead to power and wealth in fewer hands. We know that the 'old boy' network persists. We know that wealth is concentrated in few hands and even knowledge is becoming more concentrated. We have the perception that everyone has access to all the treasures, to all the poetry, science, arts that the world has to offer. Unfortunately, only a limited few exploit the wealth to enrich themselves. Most of us are slaves to Facebook or Twitter etc.

This connectivity has led to something quite dangerous in that political power is becoming concentrated in the wrong hands. The masters have learnt how to manipulate even the democratic processes to rule the multitudes. In the traditional set up lying and deceit were considered offensive. These days blatant lying happens openly, everyone is informed and perhaps as a result through some sort of malfunction in our collective behaviour we tolerate and accept it. Nigel Farage, Donald Trump, David Davis, Michael Gove, Boris Johnson, Theresa May, Amber Rudd, Jeremy Corbyn and Putin of course all tell us lies and they continue as they are. Not only is there no consequence, but their following is weirdly increased as a result.

But the backdrop to Brexit is our interpretation of what is democracy and freedom of expression. Human history is littered with people having been killed for their beliefs. Jesus Christ was a victim of preaching new faith or knowledge. Over centuries we have formulated incredible and reasonable laws. But even now in 2019 we allow the exploitation of those very laws.

There is always a counter argument or defence. Even Enoch Powel would not admit to being a racist when he was making his 'rivers of blood' speeches. But we all know that he was. And we were for the most part silent. Perhaps this is one of the key characteristics of English people. They believe themselves having certain traits and virtues. It could be 'tolerance' or 'fair play' or whatever. There is no national character. The population is as decent as any other and as silent as any other when atrocities are being committed. For the most part we are silent when a boat sinks and we have to take in some refugees into the country. We are silent when people get deported. The Windrush scandal brought us all together when it was revealed that there was a sanctioned Hostile Environment. It is all a sign of deep degradation.

My professor's wife was German. I went to stay with them once. In her moment of reflection, she wanted to convey to me that as a child she was innocent when the Jews were being rounded up in her neighbourhood. What could we do? She asked. We were helpless. If we protected them then our own lives would have been in danger. What can you do when soldiers with guns come to search your home? I had to sympathise. After all, this was an after-dinner conversation in her house.

'I can understand it,' I told her. 'You were a young girl. But your parents? They allowed you to stand at the gate and watch. Where were they?'

'They were inside,' she said.

There are different degrees of discrimination. If we remain silent, are we not also racists?

My friends argue that we are not all racists. 'Some of us just want our country back,' they say.

'And in return are we willing to give every nation their countries back?'

'Ah, they say. What do you mean?'

'I mean shall we bring back all the British people from all foreign lands? Around 10% of the British people live in other countries. Our immigrant population is also around 10% of our total population. Shall we ask all the English to come back home?'

Then there is silence.

'I want my culture and values back.'

'What is your culture and values?' I ask.

'I am English,' they say.

'What does that mean?'

More silence.

Racism is not prevalent amongst all our people. But there are many rotten apples. The young can be easily influenced. The old can change their positions by believing in a kernel of truth in the propaganda perpetuated by the *AltRight*, which in the United Kingdom is primarily represented by UKIP, The Brexit Party, the ERG and the likes of Nigel Farage and Tommy Robinson.

Modern politics is not about truths. It is a battle of ideas and brutal competition for the attention span of the crowds. Those who understand how to communicate exploit ignorance to the fullest. They exploit natural anxieties that people have about their personal lives in a competitive world, largely controlled by the needs of organisations. Organisations are also competing among themselves. Facebook with Google. Google with Microsoft. Microsoft with IBM and so on. Each is driven by not just survival, but their goal is domination. In this pursuit of getting bigger and occupying more and more of the economic space, the individual is sacrificed. The people at the very top get enormously rich. Bill Gates for example has been the richest man for quite a long time. He is worth what $120,000,000,000? People do not have any conception what that number means. His company still only pays its people the lowest salaries they can get away with. The employees are glad to have jobs. They work all the hours that God sends and at the end of the month, after tax, they receive their pay. From that pay they allocate perhaps 50% on rent in places like London. They spend 30% on food, clothing, communication, and entertainment. They spend perhaps 10% on travel. They are being diligent if they can save 10% of their gross salary. 10% of say EUR 50,000 is EUR 5,000. An apartment in place like London, Paris, Frankfurt costs around ten times average gross salaries. Banks expect 30% down payment – that is EUR 150,000. Clearly on their own they are not going to be able to save and afford home ownership.

Our country tolerates gross inequality. Historically we have been quite happy to keep the poor in their place. The modern poor are increasingly what used to be the Middle Classes. Well educated people who cannot afford a home of their own. Wealth has concentrated not only in fewer hands, but majority of wealth is concentrated in fewer cities and then within cities in a small number of locations. In London Chelsea, South Kensington, Hampstead, Highgate and one or two other localities probably have more than 40% of the residential property value of the whole of London.

This all because our government allows for free competition and does not plan investment or job creation. For more than 50 years we have allowed our financial sector to grow at the expense or neglect of manufacturing. Great Britain has had no strategy for international competition. We have watched as the Germans, Japanese and American have taken over our manufacturing base.

Great Britain remains intricately interconnected not only with Europe, but with the rest of the world. The increasing inequality between the different sections of our society has fed racism. It is just easier to blame a third party or someone who looks different for the deep problems we have created through mismanagement of our economy.

Let me give you my take on how this works. As a nation we have a crisis in the NHS. The origins of this current crisis are in the Financial Crisis of 2007/2008 which one can argue originated in the US Housing Market. That arose because a lending boom to subprime borrowers had gone on for too long and the resulting mortgages given were repackaged and sold as Investment Products. Those mortgages were not just sold outright. They were sold as leveraged products. As an example, this means mortgages of $100,000 were put into a Special Purpose Vehicle (SPV) to make up a notional of say $100m. Often the $100m was geared up by a factor of 3-5 times and $300m to $500m Notes were sold to the public. The

Notes were further leveraged by dividing the £300m into tranches. The tope tranches obtained AAA ratings from the Rating Agencies. The lower tranches, depending on how many there were, were given lower ratings. At the bottom there might be an equity tranche perhaps constituting 5% of the Notes. When only a few people defaulted on their mortgages the equity holders lost first and the lowest tranche holders, which in the absence of any defaults would have received the highest returns, lost part of their money. But when the number of defaults ended up rising, because the property values fell far below the Mortgage given, the lower tranches lost all their value. One must remember that 100% mortgages were common. When this happens, the upper tranches become relatively more risking because any further defaults end up eating up into the capital and interest payments for those investors. Property is a volatile asset class. Property values can fall by 30% quite easily in an economic downturn.

As I mentioned, at the start of the selling process the highest tranches were rated AAA – which meant that the probability of default for the topmost tranche was close to zero. The type of investors who had brought these lowest risk tranches were Pension Funds, Insurance Companies or the Issuers of these investments, which kept the safest and highest rated tranches on their own books because in the end no one wanted to buy them. Pension Funds and Insurance Companies buy safe investments because they must guarantee returns in their own business, for example they have to guarantee pensions far into the future. By the end of the process the AAA rating had to be downgraded to say BBB, where probability of losing some or significant amount of the original investment is much greater. Well as the property values fell, first the lowest tranche investors started to get out and depressed the prices, because now there were no buyers. The Pension Funds had to liquidate because they are not allowed to hold lowly rated assets in the first place. One set of losses by investors always triggers other losses because many investors themselves use leverage when investing. Panic sets in and the result was a total meltdown of financial markets with stock markets losing more than 50% of their value and many financial institutions having to be rescued.

Going back to the current problems with our NHS. As a result of the austerity the spending on the NHS has not kept up with growing demand. Austerity meant less spending on many sectors of the economy including education, transport, housing, public sector wages and so on. But let us stick to the NHS. Underfunding led to waiting lists and delays in operations. Looking for easy solutions the UKIP argument was and still is that we have too many people in the United Kingdom. Too many immigrants. They propagated that if we close our borders and either encourage or send back a lot of those immigrants our NHS would be in much better shape. Fewer people, smaller lines. But what happens when we call for the closing of our borders? The business community thinks that we are not open for business. The Polish and French workers start to make plans to go back and not invest in the UK. International businesses do not know what the rules of the game are going to be. They start either to relocate or halt their future investment plans. The result is that our economic activity and thus what our Treasury receives in the form of taxes and VAT receipts goes down. This in turn means less money for the NHS or if by squeezing more money for the NHS, then less money for Defence, Infrastructure, Housing or whatever. By waving the Union Jack we damage ourselves. For when one talks about foreigners in the third person, the foreigners sitting next to you starts to think about you as a host nation in a different way. They think that they don't have to put up with this crap and they start to make plans to either discriminate against you in return and not make you part of their lives or they decide to make plans to leave.

Our NHS would breakdown completely if it weren't in significant measure manned by foreigners, including of course second and third generation Indian, Pakistani and West Indian origin workers. Theoretically they are not foreigners. But to the average UKIP member and possibly to the average Joe Blog anyone who is not white is ultimately a foreigner.

Who becomes the focus of attention when one complains about too many immigrants? It is not the Poles or the Romanians or the French or the Italians. It is the Brown and Black people who feel intimidated. People who have lived here for fifty years, who have toiled and paid their dues and are part of the fabric of our society as teachers, doctors, nurses, pharmacists, dentists, drivers, shop keepers, street cleaners, bankers and businessmen. They get intimidated when we start to fly the Red and White English flag – for they are not English. They cannot be English. They are British.

Nationalism is of course becoming popular in Scotland, Wales, and N. Ireland. The process of devolution of powers to these governments has been going on for some time. Brexit is making the nationalistic anthem louder because Brexit is not in the best interest of these countries. But because the regions are asking for greater sovereignty, the English also want to exercise more power in England and the way to do that is to wave the English flag. Soon enough the nations across the continent of Europe want to do what is best for them and they start waving their flags and then every man is speaking only for themselves and the common good is forgotten. For me, the idea of a United Kingdom remaining united is very appealing. But if this unity comes at a cost to economic freedom and freedom of movement within Europe, my loyalty to Great Britain starts to diminish.

The Poles I have met in Hounslow are genuinely better qualified as bricklayers, painters, electricians, and plumbers compared with the skilled labour we are able to find in the local communities. The French I have met in the City of London are as good as or better risk managers compared with any other professionally qualified group of people who run our financial powerhouse. They can all resettle with minimum effort. The Polish economy is growing and in need of skilled workers. The French economy is recovering fast under Emmanuel Macron. People with skills are hard to find anywhere. We should all be grateful that they choose our country. All the reasons for them to continue to stay here or for new people to come, if diluted, would mean that we will be poorer as a result.

Let us be honest with ourselves. The origins of Brexit go back to perhaps even before WWII. The process of British withdrawal started with the realisation that the countries we were ruling over wanted us to leave, and as important, that we could not manage the Empire. 200 years of ruling India did not convert the Indian and become more like the English. They retained their religion overall and their character and even their religious divisions. Perhaps subconsciously we realised that ruling over others is an extremely hard job and we had no business doing it. The problems that faced Britain at home appeared to be insurmountable. Just a 100 years ago the poverty and squalor of British life for the many was something to be ashamed of. Great Britain had truly little to celebrate. The upper classes one can imagine have been celebrating since the Roman times.

The process of withdrawal has relentlessly continued. It is primarily through our financial institutions and industry that we have been able to keep a foot in places like Hong Kong. But a financial crisis of the scale of 2007/2008 leads to contraction and once contracted it is difficult to re-establish primacy. China is the big dragon in the room. Any vacuum left in Asia is quickly and irreversibly filled up by Chinese capital. The British influence in Asia has been diminishing for more than half a century.

Perhaps it is because we ruled over such a large part of the brown and black populations of this world that we still find it hard to treat them as equals. Most are still smaller economies. There is much we can assist them with. But being British we will want to collaborate with them on our unique terms. These terms basically translate to 'We want to do more trade, but we won't allow more of your workers in our country to make that possible.'

'Sorry Madam,' they say. 'If you want our software, you have to let our people into the country so that they can service those products.'

33

'I'll have to come back to you on that.'

'Of course, Madam. Take your time.'

Most of us do not mind them coming in, but many don't want our waiting lines for NHS get even longer. The interconnections between different parts of the economy are not analysed by UKIP supporters. The answer is not shutting the gates. The answer is to reform our NHS and invest in it to meet the needs of the population and grow the opportunities for our people. Foreigners also pay taxes. They then have the right to use the NHS.

At the same time, it is extremely difficult to manage large flow of immigrants without disruption. What else can we do?

Divorce was only a question of time

When Tony Blair first came to power, I voted for him with tears of joy. After years of Margaret Thatcher and then John Major, Tony was a voice of change for Britain. His New Labour reclaimed the centre ground. Progressive Socialism is, in my mind, when the needs of the business community are part of the overall strategy to run an efficient economy and a fair society.

Tony Blair had many faults. His approach to the economy was not a break with the past. Under Thatcher's Big Bang we got rid of a lot of regulations in the City. Our relationship with the EU evolved and London became the most important financial centre in Europe certainly if not in the world. But Thatcher's approach to politics was to cater largely to the interest of the business community at the expense of the working classes. She reduced corporate taxes, cut public services, took away free milk at schools, spent more on defence, broke the backs of Unions, and told the boys in the City to do as they pleased. Boom times were on.

I was lucky to be working in the City in the 1980's. There was a lot of innovation with the introduction of Derivatives and other Structured Products. There was huge shortage of analytical skills. Anyone who could do even basic maths calculation and work out bond yields on a calculator was already ahead of traditional bankers. If they understood what Bond Yield and the concepts of Duration, they were way ahead of the curve. If one could add the understanding cash-flows and do discounting one was really in great demand. There was so much money sloshing around in European institutions and with the Japanese. They were buying up everything. From corporate bonds with suspected ratings to Real Estate in the United States. In Investment Banks we were minting money. Correspondingly our salary increases were in double digits and one could move from job to job and expect to get twenty or thirty percent increase in base salary and perhaps double or even triple the bonus if one delivered on the numbers. By the age of 35 many working in the City had earned more than the lifetime earnings of their parents. Many brought homes and paid off the mortgage with about 5 to 7 years of income. Things were getting better for the many. Property prices were rising, and real living standards were improving. People upgraded their homes and purchased new cars and went to the Caribbean for holidays. For people working in the City the good times were to continue for quite a long time. We did not know then that the seeds of financial destruction had been laid by Margaret Thatcher and had been cultivated by Tony Blair.

But for the Tories things could not get any worse. There was much talk about having a Single Currency for Europe. The precursor to the Single Currency was what they called the European Rate Mechanism. To be part of the Single Currency the economies of members hoping to participate had to be brought into a sort of economic convergence. The way to do that was for each country over time to achieve similar economic goals. The main discipline for an aspiring country was being not having Fiscal Deficits of more than 3% of the GDP and living within their means. To achieve Convergence exchange rates were also fixed within agreed bands such that currencies could not fluctuate outside those bands. Central Banks used the leavers of changes in short term rate or interventions in the foreign exchange markets to stay within the bands.

Without going into great details, Great Britain ended up fixing the Pound's exchange rate to the Deutsche Mark at 1:4. At that exchange rate our economy simply could not compete. If the economy is not doing well the currency value is also going to decline. And it did just that. At first Nigel Lawson, who was then the Chancellor of the Exchequer, tried to defend the Pound through foreign exchange intervention. But in 1992 it was no longer sustainable, and Sterling had to be devalued. George Soros made £1,000,000,000 in profit when that devaluation happened.

What was the British folly or arrogance that led to that debacle?

It was the same old story. Our perception of ourselves has always been far grander than our capacities. We always try to punch well above our weight. Sometimes we succeed. But often the consequences are not so great and, in the end, the public picks up the pieces. This time the disconnect was with Thatcher and Nigel Lawson. Relative British productivity has been lagging for an exceptionally long time behind Germany. Yet we have always had grand visions of being able to compete with the largest economy in Europe. We won the War for God's sake. Why can't we have grade illusions? But one had to look only at the quality of cars being manufactured in Germany and compare that with what we were throwing off the assembly lines in Coventry or Dagenham to know that we were way behind. Very few countries can compete with the Germans at engineering.

The thing that we have done badly, which is having neglected investment in our future has resulted in something that we have done well. This was, perhaps out of necessity, to open doors to foreign investment. This open-door policy to foreign investment preserved and grew our workers skills. We let in foreigners not just in auto manufacturing, but in every other sector, with Financial Services being the most prominent. London in the process became perhaps the most dynamic capital in the world and the hub for trading and providing finance. Uniquely positioned with time overlapping first with Asia Pacific and Japan and then with the North American markets. We were well-endowed also with technical skills from France, Germany, and home-grown Indians and Chinese as well of course talent from our white Population. Well nurtured London has been ahead of the rest of the world in Services (Financial, Legal and Accounting) now for a whole generation.

What foreigners bring and have brought is what has kept United Kingdom afloat. The neglected family from the Midlands may see the brown man or the Japanese or the French as a threat because they feel that their lives are in a perpetual crisis but were it not for the foreigners coming and investing in United Kingdom, we may very well be a bankrupt nation by now. The reasons are obvious. We have not invested in the development of our own people. We then had to import the know-how. We opened the doors for people to come in because someone else had paid for their educations and upbringing. If one thinks about how much one spends to raise well balanced children, then one can realise what a good deal United Kingdom has had by simply opening our doors to foreigners.

There are also other reasons, with demographic being the primary one, why the countries of Europe needed to bring in foreigners. When economies grow or are operating at full employment, then industry needs more workers. Nations bring in foreign workers to fill the gaps and to keep wage inflation in check. The whole of Europe is going through demographic changes that are quite profound. We are producing fewer babies with the result that our populations are shrinking. This is so even as we live longer. The consequences of fewer young people mean that relatively there are more and more older people in the population mix. Older people are consumers of good and services not producers. The services they consume, such as NHS must be paid for by tax on the employed. One way to keep those taxes low is to bring in more people to do the work and spread out the tax burden. This is even though we need more people in work in a growing economy where governments also want to collect more in taxes so that they can spend more. Artificial Intelligence (AI) may change the need for immigrants in years to come. Robots may replace care givers. But to date that reality is not upon us and neither have we figured out how to tax robots.

Estimate of how much one needs to spend on raising kids to the age of 25 for a good education can obviously vary. My rough calculations are approximate and rather simple. 25 years is equal to 1300 weeks. On average one can spend say, £100 per week per child on food. Food alone has cost £130,

000.00. For a good education one can assume £3000 per quarter on school fees and associated expenses. Nannies when they were young. Holidays throughout. There are 100 quarters in 25 years. That comes to £300,000.00. If one apportions to each child their share of the mortgage or even rental value for the rooms they occupied and the heating bills, one can estimate they their cost was £250 per month (probably more). That comes to £75,000. This simple calculation shows that one can spend about £500,000 in raising a child to age 25, by which time they have a master's degree. Assuming we have even 2m high skilled foreign workers in our economy, one can see that £1,000,000,000,000,000.00 worth of assets that we did not pay for. No wonder that we are considering a skills-based immigration policy. We want only those people to come to Britain who have been educated at someone else's expense – fully formed and ready to work and contribute taxes. That too will not bode well for a racist Great Britain.

Brexiters resent foreigners, but don't have answers as to how the local population will cope without the teachers, doctors, nurses, bankers, engineers and shop keepers and all the spending that happens and tax that is collected from the foreign born.

Our Great Britain did not educate its people to be able to have them stand on their own feet and compete in the global environment we find ourselves in. Without foreigners we would be an extremely poor country. Much poorer compared with the Germans, French, Scandinavians, and Dutch etc. They on a relative basis have spent more money on educating, feeding, and keeping their populations healthy. But despite all the apparent differences, the whole of Europe, including the United Kingdom has 7-10% foreign born immigrants in the population mix. We in the UK have followed American trends. The worst of them imply cheap, fast foods, obesity, and poorer income distribution. Like the Americans, we have kept our poor, poor.

This neglect did not happen just under the Tories. It has happened under Labour as well. We are often just too willing to watch American manufactured entertainment. It has been easy for us because we speak the same language and for whatever reason the ties we have with America, are described as our 'special relationship.' Our musicians, actors, footballers, scientists go to America to enhance their earnings. The British (English accent) appeal to the Americans and we assume that we have a special bond. Although when one is in America there is no evidence of favouritism among them for the English. America is such a blend of nationalities and origins that the Italians, Germans, Russians, Poles, Irish, Scandinavians and obviously also the Mexicans and more recently Indians are part of their accepted norms. But then who said that love cannot be one sided? People saw Ronald Reagan admiring Margaret Thatcher and having close ties with her at a time when she was liberalising the British economy and the financial services, which the American were keen to participate in, and everyone drew the conclusion that America loved us. We were America's staunchest allies during the Cold War and up until the Wall came crumbling down in Berlin. The special relationship one can argue has roots. But there are consequences to adulation, be it at the personal or national level.

Tony Blair may have been singing the 'Cool Britannia' tune, but he did little to raise real living standards and to educate our people so that we can stand with our heads high. Tony was in a personal popularity contest. He tried to make Britons proud by having our boys fight in an unnecessary war, forged ahead by him, bending to the wishes of George W Bush, by fabricating stories about Saddam Hussein possessing Weapons of Mass Destruction. Tony either fell for the lies told by Bush or he wanted to diminish the Middle East region because Tony saw (sees) the world through his very particular Christian lenses.

If during his term as PM the money spent on unnecessary war had gone into better education, more affordable homes, more training, we probably would not have voted for Brexit. In some sectors Labour under Tony Blair did increase spending. NHS was one of them. But it was not enough. Prime Ministers want to be remembered for how great they have been. Even through each life is in a different time and goes through completely different set of circumstances and challenges, they cannot help comparing themselves with the great leaders from history. Just because they have become PM, they are obsessed with the idea of leaving behind a legacy. Well Tony Blair left a legacy. He will be remembered as the PM who at the height of his power did not know how to manage the nation and ended up deceived us all. Tony Blair did not know his own people. We do not readily forgive our leaders when they deceive us.

Our people voted for Brexit because we did not engage with Europe enough and didn't allow Europe to touch our lives. Not enough of us go to Rome, Florence, Milan, Vienna, Paris, Munich, Barcelona. Not enough of us are transformed by the rich European culture and history. Not enough of us see in that history our own glorious past, dating back to Roman times. We do not make the link and cherish the shared values, the literature, religion, history and fear the divisions that nearly destroyed us. But for many, particularly the uneducated and the old, the neglected, Europe has not touched them, and they haven't touched Europe.

When these people see a Polish man working, they see a job that they do not have and probably cannot do. But they imagine themselves doing it. They imagine it without being given the resources to have trained to do it and now without having the ability or the funding to be able to learn. They want the Pole to leave and would prefer the job not to be done. If they cannot do it, no one should. They do not see the end consequences of their jealousy, their own deprivation. They do not see the consequences for their country or even for themselves. Our imperfect democracy allows them to cast a vote, without comprehension of self-gain or self-harm.

Tony Blair, to get elected had to strike a deal with Rupert Murdock. He could have won only with the support of this right-wing Newspaper and Media Baron. The compromise or surrender of Tony Blair's values was visible from the time he started to reach out to Rupert Murdock. We should have known then that nothing good will come out of his premiership for he had compromised the values of the Labour Party at the outset.

What type of democracy we have where the outcomes are controlled by powerful and dominating media bosses? What kind of people are we if we are induced to read poisonous papers that work against our very interests?

Gordon Brown had his heart in the right place. But he did not have the support of Rupert Murdock and thus he lost to David Cameron. With the Nick Clegg's Liberals, Gordon Brown could have formed a coalition, but Nick Clegg scuppered that outcome by aligning himself with David Cameron. Gordon Brown probably did not offer him the position of Deputy Prime Minister. For the sake of personal power, Nick became part of the Tory government. Overall, one can argue that Nick Clegg had a positive impact by containing the Tories. It was only a question of time that, in power, the Tories would build up their support base while the Labour Party was in disarray after Gordon Brown stepped down and the two brothers Miliband's started to compete for the leadership of the Labour Party.

One can see that power corrupts. The focus of our politicians is to grab power and to hell with what is best for the country. In the case of the Miliband brothers, the elder brother quit politics and went to America and the younger became Leader of the Labour Party. But the Rupert Murdock machine labelled him as a back stabber of his own brother and that together with his firebrand of Socialism ruined his chances in the election. David Cameron was a fresh face. The Labour party had gone through a torturous time with first Tony Blair and Gordon Brown at each other's throats and then the Miliband brothers with their sibling rivalries competing for the same post. There were simply too many open wounds. To top it all, the financial crisis of 2008/2009 was at its peak by 2010 – at the time of the election. David Cameron and George Osborne appeared riding like White Knights to the rescue of an economy in peril. Gordon Brown had shown himself to be incompetent as a communicator and not having the backing of the media lost the country's support.

Unlike what was happening in the United States, where the Federal Reserve flushed the system with cheap money to put a floor on the collapsing economy, the new government in the UK had sold themselves as prudent Tories. They proposed cuts in public spending on a draconian scale to try and get our finances in order. Gordon Brown by 2010 had already rescued our financial system by pumping in billions of Pounds. The healing under Gordon Brown would have happened because his solutions were like the United States. The austerity measures which saw massive cuts to public spending in the NHS, welfare and education ended up really hurting the less well off. When the masses hurt, they need someone to blame. The easiest people to blame always are the immigrants.

David Cameron pressured by the Right Wing of his own party fought the second election in 2015 on a manifesto that promises a referendum on EU Membership. The referendum was held in June 2016 even though David Cameron personally was in favour of remaining in the EU. Again, to appease the extremists and to retain power David Cameron called the rather sudden referendum without having done nay homework on the possible consequences. Personally, he was convinced that the British people will vote to Remain in the EU. So convinced was he that he opted for a simple YES or NO vote. There were hardly any debates about impacts of a Leave Vote on our economy. There were no impact studies on each of the sectors of our economy. Rupert Murdock's media drilled propaganda and the Tory Leavers, lately joined by Boris Johnson fabricated lies about the saving to be had of £350 million per week that could be made available to the NHS.

The story of Brexit was not about the economy. It became a single-issue story about immigration. There were too many foreigners in our country. They were putting too much pressure on our housing, on our schools, our hospitals and they were using our services for free!

Jeremy Corbyn had won the contest for the leadership of the Labour Party after the 2015 defeat in the general election. During the time leading up to Referendum, Corbyn and the Labour Party were distinctly absent from the public debate. Labour Party itself had massive divisions after Jeremy was elected as leader. No one was willing to back his far-left socialist policies. But the young and the less well-off who had suffered under the Tories, the kids who could not afford to pay rent and were being used on Zero Hour contracts flocked to Jeremy promising free education and nationalisation of utilities etc.

Jeremy has always been ambivalent about the European Union. He has remained ambivalent since, even though there is ample and increasing evidence that leaving the EU without proper arrangements would be highly damaging for our economy.

During the referendum the Tories or the Brexiters didn't talked about the positive contribution immigrants make to the British economy. No one emphasised the taxes the foreigners paid. That their contribution in taxation exceeded what they took out in benefits. The use of free NHS by perhaps half a dozen foreigners became the kernel around which stories were built. Our hospitals had waiting lines because of the spending cuts. There were not enough doctors and nurses. There were not enough new infrastructures to meet the higher demands of an aging population. Not to say that there were not more people. British population has been rising, both due to higher birth rates and influx of new immigrants. Even if one could argue that immigrants put extra pressure on our public services, that ought to have been a hard-fought negotiation with the EU to control immigration or to decide to limit benefits to new arrivals until they start to make tax sufficient contributions. Those changes were, in fact, being implemented. Mrs. May had been working hard to control immigrant inflows. In fact, with such fervour that legally settled black people were being deported. But when the mob starts to chant, the mob acquires its own momentum. The voices can get louder and louder and with that growing certainty that the mob one is the right voice for the nation, particularly when it becomes reduced to 'us and them.' That is how Hitler consolidated his power. That is how the Japanese justified the tortures and killings. Our mob voted to leave the EU because they saw the city dwellers as the elites and themselves as the victims. There is quite a lot of truth in that. The EU had nothing to do with it!

We voted to leave in regions where the white immigrant populations from the EU are not significant. People in the Midlands, North and North East voted to leave. They thought that the government would control or deport brown immigration. They wanted the Commonwealth origin brown and black people to be thrown out. Surprisingly in addition, the brown men and women from these regions also voted to leave. They did so because they thought white boys from Poland, Hungary and Romania were coming to displace them.

White working-class who don't have European friends, who cannot distinguish between our and European culture, have not benefited from Free Movement voted for Brexit.

Of course, the men and women sitting in the Midlands, getting paid the minimum wage or without jobs were saying to themselves, 'yes, if only the government was not spending all that money on foreigners, putting recently arrived boat people in hotels, we would be better off – because the government is then bound to redirect those savings to us.' £350 million a week would go into the NHS. No more waiting for hip replacements. Britain would reclaim its glorious past. We will have a Global Britain and reengage with the rapidly developing nations such as India, Indonesia, former colonies in Africa and China. Everything will work out perfect and we'll be free from the stranglehold of the EU. All those contributions we make to the EU budget, will be able to spend as we please. Hardly anyone understood that while we were making contributions, the EU was investing huge sums in regeneration of the less developed parts of the United Kingdom. Our net contributions were insignificant compared to the economic benefits of membership.

 Theresa May promptly paid a visit to Mr. Modi. Liam Fox trotted off to Australia, New Zealand, and Canada – all the white nations first in the hope of signing multiple trade deals. He thought it would all be a simple 'cut and paste' job using the agreements with the EU already in place as the template. Two years on, not a single new trade agreement has been signed. The reasons are obvious. Great Britain is not the EU. We cannot reciprocate in the same way as the combined economies of the largest economic block on the planet. And if we cannot, our trading partners want something more from us. We don't have much else to give, other than, either opening our borders to more foreigners or to open our markets for products which we may not want to accept – such as chlorinated chicken from the United States or children exploited shirts from Indian factories.

The hopeful illusions of the poor never cease to amaze. The beggar in the street assumes that the more money the rich have, the more they are likely to donate to them. In fact, the rich do not give to people in need. It is the average person who is more likely to throw a quid into the stretched hand of the needy. The rich just keep more of the money they have, sometimes earning nothing and doing nothing with it. The rich despise the poor for occupying the space in our streets. The hard ERG Tory type rich think that people beg because they are lazy and unwilling to work!

Theresa May and her Cabinet Clowns

It is cold and wet Wednesday in October 2018. I am watching PMQ.

Theresa May is a vicar's daughter. She is a year younger than me. I point this out to illustrate that one can grow up in the same era but end up having a completely different political ideology. We create our own realities based on our set of circumstances. The England I grew up in is not the same as Theresa May's England.

My father was not a vicar. But he too was extremely religious. The more I learnt about science, the less religious I became, until I became an atheist. This vicar's daughter is still the vicar's daughter.

Theresa May, our Prime Minister, did not want to leave the EU. But throughout the referendum process she did not actively campaign to stay. She was hedging her bets. If the vote had been to remain, David Cameron would still be PM and she would still be Home Secretary. As it turned out David Cameron lost and promptly resigned. The Party chose Mrs. May to be PM. There was no one else credible. Boris Johnson had his supporters, but he is bit of a clown. During the campaign Boris had been hedging his bets also. For quite some time he was undecided on the EU. He was not sure if he was for Remaining or Leaving. Eventually Boris Johnson did what he thought would be best for Boris Johnson. He chose to join the Leave campaign.

Boris Johnson travelled on the big red bus with the bold message: 'We send the EU £350 million a week, let's fund our NHS instead. Vote Leave. Let's take back control.'

Framed in that way and with so much discussion on waiting times for operations in our hospitals and the media's focus on immigration the support for Leave build up. Still, it was a surprise result. Sterling collapsed from around £1.45 against the dollar to under £1.20.

Some people have been infatuated by Boris Johnson and think that he is very clever. He certainly has had a privileged education. He is well read, and he can twist and turn the English language. And he can make bold untruthful statements and then later retract or trivialise them. Boris Johnson often talks to impress rather than having substance. We also admire people who make fun of others. Boris is one of those characters who can at his whim pick on immigrants and describe them in derogatory terms and be very offensive. The English just love such characters because Boris Johnson ends up saying what even decent English people want to say but suppress it.

Michael Gove started off supporting Boris Johnson for the Tory leadership contest but was later quite traitorous and backstabbed Boris Johnson and put forward his own name as a contestant. Michael Gove said: 'Boris on reflection, didn't have the personality to be PM.'

Mrs. May won by a large majority and became PM in 2016. As Home Secretary she was aware of the pressures that immigration was causing and keenly aware that for the British people immigration has been a vexing issue for quite some time, but particularly so since 2010. The influx of both EU and non-EU immigration had been above numbers targeted and promises made by the Tories under David Cameron. Why the targets were there in the first place, given that we are part of the EU, which has free movement as a core right at the heart of being a member? The targets were there to appease the far-right gang in the Conservative Party and to deceptively win support from the Shires. Making immigration an issue in British politics is a game politician play on both sides of the political divide.

The new government's key task became making Brexit happen. In hindsight it is clear to say that no one had a clue about the consequences of that 52% Leave vote. No one was prepared. The first response of the markets was as if the country had been hit in the face with a cricket bat. Overnight imports were going to be 20% more expensive.

The FTSE 100 jumped, rather than crashing. People thought that things were not so bad after all. But few understand that the FTSE 100 is made of either foreign companies listed on the stock exchange or British companies that do majority of their business in overseas markets. When the Pound goes down in value, the foreign earnings of those companies translate to more Pounds. As a result, the share prices in Pounds goes up.

Mrs. May created the position of a Brexit Secretary and appointed the Leaver, David Davis to the role. Boris Johnson was appointed as the Foreign Secretary; an astute move at one level, making the Brexiters responsible for the implementation. But Boris had said many rude things about Europe and the leaders in Brussels. They were not going to then accept him with open arms. In fact, one doubts if any world leader takes Boris Johnson seriously. Everyone knows that Boris Johnson cannot be trusted. When an appointed Foreign Secretary cannot be trusted then the United Kingdom cannot be trusted. The only countries that pretended to give Boris an audience are those where Boris was promoting their agenda. Those countries are Israel, Saudi Arabia and of course Trump's America. Boris is not credible in the whole of Europe, much of Africa and Asia.

David Davis proved, since Brexit, to be totally incompetent. He went to his first meeting without any preparations and was misleading the nation about Sector Impact Studies. First, he claimed that his team had put together impact studies on 50-odd sectors and then admitted that no such thing existed. There were all sorts of heroic stories being bandied about David Davis. It was reported that he walked blind-folded over a ledge of a castle which has a 50-foot fall. One misstep and he would be dead. The only conclusion I drew from his folly is that David Davis is a reckless man. He is quite happy to step into the dark without knowing the consequences.

Mrs. May was seen to be steadier but has proved to be as incompetent. She has used all kinds of slogans, such as 'Brexit means Brexit', 'We are prepared to have a No Deal instead of a Bad Deal', or 'We are willing to walk away.' It is difficult to know if she believed in everything she said or she was reciting what had been forced down her throat by the likes of David Davis, who threatened to resign each time he didn't get his way.

They have been and are all bluffers. They overestimate how important the United Kingdom is. They do not comprehend that Europeans care little about our impetuous behaviour. After years of hearing complaints and threats about Britain leaving the EU, many Europeans are not so unhappy about Brexit. British arguments that show our confidence that we are the 6th largest economy and that we have a trade deficit with the EU and that they thus need us more than we need them have had no impact. Of course, a hard Brexit will hurt European jobs and growth. But now in the summer of 2018, European growth is in rude health – particularly German economic growth. Unemployment is under three percent. Industry is operating at near full capacity. And it is not Boris Johnson who decides which car or Washing machine consumers buy. People who can afford German cars do so because Germany produces some of the best automobiles in the world. In their segment, no other manufacturer competes with BMWs, Mercedes, or Volkswagens. The Germans now own the best of British Car Brand – the Mini. Jaguar is owned by an Indian company, Tata Motors. The only great British success story in manufacturing of the last twenty years has been Dyson and Arm Holding. The latter has been taken over by Softbank Group, a Japanese company.

Looking at basics, the EU has 27 members. The risks of Britain leaving are dispersed over 27 countries in terms of negative consequences for them. The risks posed to Britain have to be absorbed by our one not so United Kingdom.

Is Mrs. May the PM we needed for these times? This is a complex question. Any leader is limited by the quality of people around them. Britain has had the misfortune of having perhaps the most incompetent ministers in charge in a generation. The mess Mrs. May left behind as Home Secretary, what with forced deportations of the Windrush generation was inherited by Amber Rudd. She proved to be equally discriminatory and incompetent in dealing with that crisis.

In a tranquil environment they may have pulled things off. In complex negotiations bluster simply does not deliver. How do we remain relevant if our starting point when dealing with 27 is to tell them that they need us as much as we need them? There are a couple of countries with which we do more trade than others. Other than that, on average EU members individually need UK 1/27th less than we need the EU if one just counts the number of countries. True, the UK economy is bigger than most. The adverse impact on the UK may only be 10 times as much.

The stark reality of Brexit is not £350 million per week in savings we shall make by leaving the EU, but the more than £350 million per week in losses due to worse outcomes for UK business. Every single sector of the economy will be worse off. So many businesses have put new investments on hold. So many manufacturing companies have threatened to relocate to EU countries. The financial sector is already relocating to Dublin, Frankfurt, Paris, Luxembourg, Malta, or Barcelona.

The EU may not allow financial services 'Passport Rights' to distribute financial products across the member states – because our regulations will diverge, and we will not have the exact same laws as the European Court of Justice (ECJ) and thus not the same investor protection.

A significant part of our manufacturing base is foreign owned. In the Auto Sector, BMW, Daimler, Ford, GM, Nissan, Toyota, Tata Motors etc. manufacture in the UK for the domestic market, but also to export. Airbus and Bombardier are EU and foreign owned. Britain has been an attractive destination for Pharmaceutical, Chemicals, Energy, Water and Agriculture industries. We are good at innovation across all sectors. But we have not been so great at manufacturing, even though our workers have the skills. Even if we were more like Japan or South Korea or Germany, we'd want to be able to sell in foreign markets. On all accounts being a member of the EU is better for us.

Our Financial Services side-lined capital flows into the manufacturing sector since the time of Margaret Thatcher's Big Bang. At present 70% of our economy is Services. In addition to banking, trading and dominating in global finance, our domestic economy is all about flipping hamburgers and serving.

The incompetents possibly have a hidden agenda. We have seen how small 'countries' such as Hong Kong, Singapore and Switzerland have thrived. Switzerland is part of the EEA and thus in many respects part of the EU. But the thriving part has a lot to do with how the economic model in each country is optimised. The citizens of these three countries are much better educated on average compared to our people. The governments have spent a lot of money on public infrastructure. This makes their economies a lot more efficient. Spending priorities are such that individual and corporate taxes are lower. This results in high savings rates. We want to be able to mimic their success, but we are unable to shed our colonial heritage and perceive ourselves as 'powerful' on the global stage. That requires us to have nuclear weapons, war ships and the latest military hardware and the BBC to keep alive our soft power. Our arrogance has no bounds. We are still interested in shaping the world, even when we don't, any longer, have the means and are really very tired.

The extremist ERG membership Tories want to have a hard Brexit. That means virtually breaking all meaningful ties with Europe. They want Great Britain to be turned into a low 'Tax Offshore Centre' for the world's rich to bring their capital. They want to relax regulations around Money Laundering and turn our economy into 'anything goes'. That may still happen. But what are the consequences?

The consequences of turning our backs on Europe are far reaching. As Islands we have never felt European. Our links with the Commonwealth and our perceived close relationship with the United States has given us false comfort that we have another place in the world. Forgetting that we are first and foremost European and trying to cause divisions between our neighbours by arousing anti-EU sentiments has become a national past time. It is difficult to comprehend what benefit we derive by undermining our friends? It is not in the national interest to divide. Our actions are visible to the Europeans. They can read and understand our language. We have some world class newspapers that are read all over the world. Our BBC is the envy and source of balanced reporting across the globe. The behaviour of our politicians is visible to everyone and as a nation we have become the laughingstock. All the uproars of PMQ and the pedestal we give to the likes of Nigel Farage, is a poor reflection on our democracy.

The Leavers believe that our open-door policies have been the root cause of Brexit. People were complaining about foreigners influencing our destiny. In their eyes most of these foreigners who have control over our destiny reside in Brussels. They impose on us their rules, even though we are part of the common rules making process. The EU forces us to follow minimum safety standards, govern our policies around workers' rights, environment, and human rights etc. The list goes on and on. And we are fed up with it, they say. We are a sovereign nation, and we should have our own laws.

It does not matter if our own laws are inferior or backward looking. We just do not want anyone else telling us what to do. Given the glorious past we come from it is not unusual that we should hanker for that greatness again. But greatness must be sustained in the qualities of our people. That means we must invest in them and make them among the most accomplished. There was a time that a small minority could innovate and lead. Many working-class factory workers underneath a manager or two did the menial tasks and the whole economy was successful. The days of a few discoveries which gave us a massive lead in the global economy are over. Not only is competition far fiercer, but innovation and invention must now happen along the whole supply chain. British workers have mainly been trained by foreign employers. We have left it to Nissan to set up the most efficient assembly lines. Britain has failed its citizens because we have not invested in them. Unlike the Germans and the Japanese, we have been too ready to fire them as soon as we did not need them. We are far more ruthless with our people. Far less caring. Where does this originate?

One can observe that our political system that still relies on having the Queen as our Head of State side by side our elected Members of Parliament and an unelected chamber of the House of Lords. Our system reflects how we are conditioned to keep a sense of place in our society. With that higher order we have long accepted and tolerated social inequality. The world of upstairs and downstairs is part of our accepted inheritance. No matter how we try to dress it up, the reality is that the rich don't care about the poor. They are more interested in keeping them in their place. That in the end is the tragic part of British life. Our nation is always struggling because we have for so long accepted and have normalised inequality in our society. We actively deny our people opportunities and then wonder why we are being left behind as a nation.

One measure of how equal we are across the board is to look at how affordable it is to have access to our high culture. How many working-class people in Britain can enjoy our Theatres and Operas? How many can afford the tickets and the cost of dinner in London's best restaurants? How many don't even give a toss because they much rather be watching another football match and wearing their club's shirts and wave little flags?

One can argue that our democracy is less functioning because we have greater inequality between the rich and the poor. Relatively our working classes are worse off compared with the working classes of many European countries. Ours are less well educated and poorer. But democracy is one of the keyways in how we define ourselves. It is as if we swallowed a 'democracy pill' and believe in it without evidence.

These are all causes of Brexit. When Boris Johnson talks about Brexit, he is talking only about how he sees it for himself and the class he comes from and represents. His views have been formed at *The Spectator* – a right wing publication. Boris Johnson doesn't understand the needs of the working poor. If he sincerely did, he would not be supporting Brexit. But then again, he has been ambivalent about Europe. He has done what suited him at the time. For some time, he supported or appeared to support David Cameron and then at the last-minute Boris shamelessly switched sides. Then perhaps that is what power is all about. It is about self-promotion. What is surprising is that our people don't get it. They keep reading *The Sun* or *The Mail* and they keep voting for these charming politicians who limit their prospects.

Writer's block

I ended up having a writer's block. One can go into all kinds of reasons why Brexit is happening and consequences for Great Britain. One can talk about the divisions Brexit is creating in our society and parts of UK. The interests of Wales, Northern Ireland, Scotland and within the UK the divergent interests of immigrants, the white people who have been left behind, the older generation and the young, the educated and the less well educated and the uneducated and their prospects as Europeans or as Brexiters. Because all these issues have been discussed to death in the media, it would make for boring reading and thus I did not know how to continue.

For the last two weeks I have not written anything. I have switched off from Twitter also because the only feeds I get on Twitter are the feeds that reinforce my own views. It is all same, same each day. And that is also uninspiring.

I do not want to go back into history and try and justify the current reality we are facing. History is history and the here and now is the culmination of the choices we have collectively made. And I know that even the present has many perspectives and thus we experience own present and its unfolding and thus have our very own sense of what is history. Even if we all know and share the knowledge that someone by the name of Margaret Thatcher was the Prime Minister of the United Kingdom in the 1980's and that she was known as the Iron Lady, our perception of that era or indeed of the PM is different depending on our own personal history. I came from a poor background and absolutely hated what she did. Others felt liberated by her policies. And if those years witnessed a rise in overall living standards which may have had nothing to do with Margaret Thatcher, we still want to credit her because it was during that time Britain finally started to become more prosperous, even though the onset of economic growth could have been explained by multiple other factors which had very little to do with what was going on in the United Kingdom. Global trade was making all participants wealthier.

We are going through such an experience now. Global growth is happening in a synchronous way ten year after the biggest financial crisis the world witnessed. Because finally we are seeing growth and a rise in stock markets everywhere and because for many their net worth is increasing, be it in due to rising prices of the properties they live in or because they finally have a job or because they are invested in the stock markets or because they have a Pension Plan, we are all feeling rather good. In the case of Brexit Britain, even though our growth is now lagging, but the mere fact that our fortunes are also rising means that we are less unhappy about our prospects. Because Brexit has not resulted in pain, we assume that it is not as damaging.

Ultimately Brexit may not end up being so damaging. That still does not mean that it is good for us. The question is how is Brexit going to change us as a people? Are we bigger or smaller personalities in isolation? I have relatives living in the Punjab. They have their land, and they have their tractors and servants. But the reality of their lives is that they cannot relocate to London or Zurich because they are uneducated and they don't have the savings to make the move and most importantly they don't have the education and language skills to make success of any move they might even contemplate. Even if they contemplated a move, it is unlikely that they will get a Visa. That is exactly what we are giving up in the UK, we are giving up our choices when we are in a fortunate position to have them.

Let us take the extreme view. All this mobility that EU permits, who does it benefit? It benefits the few people who are mobile. The vast majority must cope with their circumstances. If born in Birmingham, they are stuck with Birmingham or are tied to Birmingham. That means their interest is making

Birmingham a better place to live. The question then is, can Birmingham be made to function to serve just the British economy? Or does Birmingham and its residents have international ambitions of their own? Do they want to conquer the world of trade and finance beyond the boundaries of Birmingham? If they do, would their lives not be so much easier if they could have freedom of movement and freedom to set up their offices wherever they chose? Is the world already not very small with the likes of Amazon and Facebook breaking national boundaries? On LinkedIn I end up getting people from Brazil to Mexico, Hong Kong to Australia, India to Poland wanting to connect. Why? Because they see benefits of access, of being able to exchange ideas and information. And we are choosing to shut ourselves off!

Whichever avenue I explore I feel that I arrive at a dead end. We have in Mrs. May perhaps the least capable Prime Minister in a generation. It does not matter that she is dogged and carries on. She has been sticking to her guns. Even though every scenario, every respectable economic forecast shows that a No Deal Brexit would cause great disruptions and harm, Mrs. May will not say that No Deal is off the table.

She doggedly goes on also because there is no other choice. There is no other viable leader in the Conservative Party who would do a better job of Brexit. Brexit is a dog's dinner. The best deal will be worse than simply calling it a day and Remaining in the EU.

The softest of Brexit, some say, may end up not being so bad. If it indeed turns out to be not so bad Mrs. May will get some credit for it. But the pro Europeans won't give up. Neither will the anti-Europeans. Britain will remain divided and this journey into the future has a long way to go.

That is why I have my writer's block when it comes to telling the story of a very English Brexit. No matter what sins against our collective interests Boris Johnson commits, the reality is that he is still there the next day. There is a part of the media that loves him and there is a large part of the population that will forgive him, not matter what – all because at least for now they have their jobs and they know that he makes no difference to their lives and then why not simply support the joker they have become accustomed to. We have very low expectations from our politicians. It has reached a point that if they are mildly entertaining, we are happy to vote for them. It is like sitting in a canoe in a gently flowing river. We are happy to drift along carefree because for many our small world is enough. Perhaps it ought to be for many more.

Perhaps globalisation is tiresome. What is its objective? Why do we have to participate? Were we not better off in an all-White Britain? Wasn't life much easier simply having the class structure and knowing our place in our society? Social mobility has been a goal but only a few have ever participated. The boys and girls from Derby certainly are not participating in social mobility and swapping their positions with the upper crust. Why do we have to in addition cope with the Pakistani's, the Muslims, Indians, and the Romanians?

I can understand every point of view. Even the Indian in Britain do not want the Poles and the Hungarians. They do not want them to be crowding them out of Hounslow.

Looking at Brexit from a purely personal and selfish viewpoint, I too am for it. I do not want unwanted foreigners as neighbours. I want to be able to travel freely and be able to sell my products and services wherever I please. I do not want to be accountable to anyone in how I run my life. I want my own rules and my own laws and within my own borders I should be allowed to do as I please. I want you to buy the services I offer from London, but I do not want you to be able to come to London to sell your services. I want to choose who I let in. Do you see why I am getting confused? I do not understand our stance. I am having a bloody writer's block.

47

Incompetence all around and I have a writer's block.

British Culture and Values

There is no question that once upon a time Britain was great. There is no question that Britain remain a great Union of four nations. Past greatness is over. The empire is lost. The union is on very shaky grounds. Perhaps it is best that we prepare for the day when the four members of the unions are genuinely independent nations, and we move away from talking about Great Britain and refer to the four countries by name. I can see this happening when I project forward. Brexit is likely to accelerate the demise of Great Britain and with that it will be difficult to talk about British Values.

I see that as a good development, for the English are quite distinct from the Irish, Welsh, and Scots. There is no such thing as 'British values.' Our uniqueness comes from the land mass we occupy and our history and culture. Histories are always unique to individuals as well as nations. The big sweep of it are our victories and losses. Our literature and art. Although with literature and art, the more it is shared, the less claim we have on it. Shakespeare, Dickens, and Turner have lessons for anyone who is cultured. Great values, like great cultures get dispersed. One can be sure if there is anything uniquely English or Indian and has not be adopted by others, it isn't worth having.

There is no denying that some of the first scientific discoveries were made here. Britain was for quite a long time the leading industrial nation in the world. That rich history and dominion over others has left its mark on the British character. Nations define themselves from the things they have accomplished, whatever those things are. The folklore results and is repeated. The recited history is the only thing that is unique about a people – their link to that string. Our collective character, if there is such a thing, is the end amalgamation of the retention of that history that we carry in each one of us. Quite often our collective consciousness is more myth than fact. Among Sikhs, we have folklore that our brave continues to destroy the enemy even after their own heads have been chopped off. King Arthur is possibly the equivalent English myth.

Great nations can become ordinary in only a generation or two if they do not remain diligent and stay on the right path. Just because we invented, and we were great once and explored the world and exercised our diplomacy and power does not guarantee our continued relevance. To remain relevant, we must make practical our ingenuity and not repeat the errors of the past. We must adjust to our current situation and the possibilities and options that generates for us.

We have every reason to be proud of our history. We must widen the selective memory of it that makes us believe in who we are. We must repaint in our imagination not what we have been told about Churchill and the British empire but be prepared to look at everything afresh from the opposite side and with a broader view. Britain may have had the greatest empire, but we have left most of our people in neglect as second-class citizens. Yes, they heard stories of our greatness, but very few participated in any meaningful way. Also, are we unique as a result? Are we in some ways a special people? Are we exceptional? Do we have unique traits and values not to be found elsewhere? The answer is most definitely not. The perception that either Christianity or the civil service introduced to our colonies helped them and that alone was enough of a gift for the two hundred years of rule should not wash. We need to come to terms with the reality of exploitation and mistreatment, including slavery. Even when your own children grow you must start treating them like adults with full rights. The conquered have largely grown up. Development is still needed, but they are not lesser people in any sense.

We certainly have some great success resulting from our history. We have the English language. We borrow words and phrases from all over the world and adopt them to make our language rich, subtle, and complex. We share our language with so many in the world and in fact to such an extent that it is no longer just ours. The Chinese and Japanese have done with knowledge and technology what we have done with language. They have taken 'our knowhow' and turned it into widgets better than we could manage ourselves. They have leapfrogged us in manufacturing and created the instruction manuals in English. One can argue that the Indian have caught up with literary talent.

Whatever it is was that made us control the seas, air and land masses in the 19th Century and made us great then, is no longer our reality. Simply having a link to greatness is not good enough in a globally connected and competing world. Japan, Hong Kong, Singapore, Australia, Canada, United States and much of Europe is either ahead of us or on par. China is leaping ahead and India is perhaps only 30 years behind. Britain is a relatively small landmass, with a relatively small population, with a medium sized economy that has been slipping for the last 40-years. It is time to pack away our snobberies and do a reality check.

Like most countries, the people we are, is largely the religion we have practiced for centuries. The Hindus are unique because they believe in many Gods. We are unique because we believe in the one, we do. Historically the scriptures and myths were important. These are the anchor of our self-belief and righteousness. The battle cry is always the life after death visions, country, and honour. Certainly, the two wars consolidated our belief in ourselves and confirmed that we can win over the odds. But we don't give enough credit to the support and sacrifices that were made by our colonies and the help we received from America. We like to claim that it was all Churchill's doing. Only his vision and only his tenacity. Help from our friends and combination of intellect and luck may have played an important part in our historical victories. For believers, the idea of God gets reinforced. But to assume that we can go it alone in any circumstances and at any time is the self-harming belief of a gambling nation. To have faith in 'always winning against the odds' is a trait of a highly irresponsible people.

Many countries are managed this way. Perhaps for individuals also, ambition often exceeds capabilities. The rewards of being first to discover are worth the gamble. But one should make sure that one can throw the dice many times. In any event, God and our belief in miracles has continued to diminish over the last 40-years. This is not just true in Britain, but everywhere. Economic growth, and added personal security has a lot to do with it. When one is not in need, there is no need for God. If not that, then the creation of life in a test tube has demystified life itself. Genetic engineering, artificial limbs, organs transplants have all contributed to loss of faith in God – everywhere. Then of course great scientists, like Steven Hawking put the last nails in the coffin of God as the creator of everything. Creation it turns out just happens. The universe emerges from nothing and submerges into nothing. We, the human species, and life on earth generally is a simple by product of the elements and an improbable set of conditions. Given the vastness, all possible spectrum of conditions most likely prevail in innumerable spots in the universe.

The history of empire has left with an 'us and them' mentality in Britain. Race relations are better now than they were 30-years ago. We are a tolerant people. We are an honest race, we are told. This is an imperial and fake legacy. Tolerance, honesty, faith, fairness are not uniquely British virtues. In fact, no virtues or conditions are unique to a nation. Indians who moved to the United States 40-years ago have become Americans for most practical purposes. They may still be taking off their slippers when they enter their prayer rooms, but they come back to the dumb TV commercials and order Big Macs and Fries with large Cokes just like all the white folks. They are just as obese. For the most part they think the same thoughts and dream the same dreams. A country can have 1,000 years of history, but if one brings in new immigrants and they can live in harmony and their children exposed to the result of that 1,000 history, like Guinee pigs, they will make that their normality. Even I have started to call Britain my country, the

British my people. What else have I to define me after 50 years of living in London and struggling through life?

Blacks, Indian and Pakistanis are no longer content with patronising attitudes of the English. No longer content with 'greater equality.' Nothing less than equality will suffice. There is nothing special about being off white and English. As far as my children are concerned it is just an accident of birth and pigmentation.

Football and Fish and Chips is now shared globally. Even Christmas dinners, crumpet, pork pies are found in farfetched places. Our music, literature, theatre, comedy has been internationalised. John Lennon was killed in New York. Everyone loves the Beatles. They don't belong just to us. We need to be less possessive about our history. It impacted others and left imprints. It is also their history.

Everyone has read and watched Macbeth and Romeo & Juliet. Andrew Lloyd Weber is loved the world over. Steven Hawking belongs to the people who understand his works. Nothing British about him, except to say that this soil, for all its drawbacks does nourish genius. But genius is not something that can be wrapped in flags. It's not ours alone. In fact, in a global village, national character becomes meaningless. Personal character and individual skills are what really counts. Knowledge and information and putting those to use counts above everything else.

Nothing here needs to stop us from competing, succeeding, or leading wholesome lives. One does not need special values or virtues to innovate, to be creative, to be funny, to sing, to market or to tell good stories. Ultimately life is about being able to tell a good story as life unfolds or when looking back. If each of us concentrates on making a good story of our personal lives that will result in success for our families, our communities, and our nation.

Given the above, Brexit will not preserve anything. Culture is not a jar of pickle that one can close the lid on and preserve. Unshared, cultures fade. Unnourished by new blood cultures crumble and vanish.

Mrs May's deal

Mrs. May has negotiated the Withdrawal Agreement with the EU. She negotiated hard. The WA will allow us to:

- control our borders

- put an end to free movement and allow Britain to control the type of emigrants who can come and live in Britain

- allows to take control of our laws by ending the jurisdiction of the European Court of Justice (ECJ)

- we don't have to pay into the EU budgets

- control of our waters and thus who can fish in our water

- no hard border between Northern Ireland and the Irish Republic in line with the Good Friday Agreement

- we can sign our own trade deals around the world

Mrs. May has been cherry picking. She has come up with a 'Soft Brexit'. But the softness is such that it leaves Britain half in and half out. But that was to be expected if we want to trade on the best possible terms and collaborate on security, research, climate change etc. That was to be expected if we want to have unfettered market access. We then must be willing to pay for the benefits.

To assure that there will never be a hard border in Ireland, the agreement has what they call a 'Backstop'. This Backstop permits good and people to move freely without border checks and controls indefinitely. If the technology solutions are not in place to permit movement without checks and controls at the border during the transition period, then current conditions will continue.

This is all extremely tricky because for as long as the Backstop is there, essentially N. Ireland remains part of the EU, but the rest of Britain will be outside.

It is a 585-page document which is meant to govern our future relationship, even though what is finally agreed, hopefully will happen during the transition period through hundreds of treaties.

For trade to flow freely between any two regions the items that are being traded must comply with local standards on both sides. This applies to product quality, guarantees, safety standards. In the case of medicines, for example, the dosages and shelf life of products must come with consumer standards and appropriate health warning.

This is important even for countries outside the EU. If Britain is trading with China, our companies will have to either adopt wholesale EU standards or come up with British standards that will then need to be agreed with the Chinese. If British standards when trading with the Chinese will be lower, then our manufacturers may have to produce two sets of the same underlying product, one for the EU market and one for the Chinese market. Best would be to just keep the same EU standards that we have now.

What is proposed on immigration is that Free Movement will be replaced with merit-based immigration policy. We'll give work permits according to the needs of the economy. Perhaps like Singapore and Australia, Britain will introduce work permits. People can stay for as long as they have jobs. Perhaps it will end up being more drastic as is the case in much of the Middle East. People won't have the rights to own property. Foreign workers will not be able to bring their families. In Singapore and Hong Kong, the domestic workers, predominantly female, clean homes, and baby sit during the day and are lonely at night. They send their savings as foreign exchange remittances but remain separated from their loved ones for years. In Oman, where I was recently, the male to female ratio is 100 to 89. There are lot of Pakistani and Indian men working in hotels or in the construction industry in Oman, in addition to the bias at birth.

There are huge risks. The racist elements in Britain, as I have argued in these pages, will end up being terribly upset if white Europeans are replaced by brown immigrants and the percentage of the brown population starts to increase substantially.

Mrs. May knows and admits that her deal is not as good as what we already have with the EU purely based on economic considerations. But she says and the Brexiters believe that the price is worth paying for the sake of democracy. The argument she is making is that Parliament voted to hold a Referendum in 2016. A lot of people turned up to vote. The people voted to Leave, and we must implement the will of the people no matter what.

Mrs May acknowledges that there were flaws with the referendum. However, she is adamant in delivering Brexit. Britain, she repeats, will leave the EU on March 29, 2019.

This is all rather sad. For the first time in history a nation is choosing to be poorer and choosing to have overall worse laws and regulations for its citizens and yet wants to describe itself as democratic. It is as if we are living through some sort of reality warp. On our TV screens people who are intelligent and well educated tell us blatant lies. There is a 'Leave Means Leave' campaign supported by Nigel Farage with many well-respected MPs and business leaders. There are radio programs on LBC with relatively new personalities or personalities that I had never paid attention to before who simply lie through their teeth. Nationalism has a very ugly side to it.

Nicola Sturgeon, the First Minister of Scotland has been fighting fiercely to remain. She knows that Scotland will be damaged outside the EU, not only because the EU acts to neutralise the powers from London. Important for Scotland is that the country continues to attract EU workers and investments. Sadiq Khan, the mayor of London sees obvious benefits for the City's services.

All living past Prime Ministers, Tony Blair, John Major, Gordon Brown, David Cameron are on the remain side. BoE Chancellors are divided with Nigel Lawson, who now lives in France and has apparently applied for a French Passport, is on the Leave side. Mark Carney the present governor of BoE has warned about the negative economic impacts of a No Deal Brexit. Mervyn King is for Brexit. Gordon Brown is pro-EU. The ghosts of Edward Heath, Margaret Thatcher is often revoked as pro-Europeans. Michael Heseltine is so angry with the current Tory party that he can hardly conceal his anger. He thinks that Brexit is mad. Kenneth Clarke is a supporter of Remain. But he is willing to compromise and respect the result of the referendum.

The BBC appears to have lost its neutrality. Newsnight and Andrew Marr get accused of pro Brexit bias. BBC is often inviting Nigel Farage, John Redwood and, Jacob Rees-Mogg - a childlike MP, who chairs the European Research Group (ERG) - extreme right wing of the Conservative Party. This lot are pushing for a No Deal Hard Brexit, where Britain will virtually cut off all formal ties with the EU and trade on WTO Rules. A huge amount of work has been done by the Bank of England and the Treasury on the impacts of a Hard Brexit. It is widely accepted that a Hard Brexit will result in most damage, with house prices crashing by up to 1/3 and, the Pound collapsing and our GDP growth being reduce significantly over the next 10-15 years.

What is motivating these Leavers? What are they hoping to gain? Is it a long-term strategy for our country to flourish or are they like vultures, waiting for chaos to ensue so that they can pick up UK assets on the cheap? I don't understand their motivations. They don't say why they have become the enemies of the EU. It is not, I am sure, as simple as restoring British sovereignty. I suspect that something else is afoot. Some drivers of change that I cannot see. I don't understand a person like Tommy Robinson. What drives him? Is it money? Is it patriotism? Is it simply the desire to be known?

There are a lot of minor players. Sajid Javid, the Home Secretary comes across as inflated by his position. Having risen in the Tory ranks, he is willing to blindly push forward the Tory agenda just to prove that he is worthy. Mr. Javid knows that he would be labelled a traitor as soon as he steps out of line. He is going to do his best not to.

Mrs. May won a vote of No Confidence motion by 200 to 117 of Tory MPs. The motion was organised with the help of the ERG. Even though they lost, the extremists continue to ask that Mrs. May resign. Another No Confidence vote cannot now be held for 12-months. She has promised to step down before the next election but is adamant in delivering Brexit in one form or another.

It is fair to say that Parliament is divided. Labour would like to have a general election. If a general election is not granted then 'all options are open', including a Peoples Vote with the option to remain in the EU.

SNP wants to remain and supports a People's Vote, while the DUP is not so sure. DUPs only stance is that N. Ireland should not be used as a bargaining chip, and that whatever happens, there must not be different rules applying to N. Ireland compared to the rest of Great Britain. The SNP also wants a level playing field, viewing that if N. Ireland is given preferential treatment in terms of EU access then same should apply to Scotland.

Our nation is divided along all possible lines. Families and friends, the old and young, north and south, educated and less well educated, locals and foreign origin are on opposing sides. The Union is in disarray. These divisions are unlikely to be healed, irrespective of where we end up.

Holding the Brexit referendum was the worst decision in British politics in a long time. I do not blame David Cameron because I know that he was not and is not bright enough to have envisaged the consequences. Anti-EU sentiment had been simmering for ages. No one corrected the lies and falsehoods. Everyone used it for their own political ends.

British politics is dysfunctional. We have the worse media in Europe. Our journalistic standards have been so low that we consume the output in the same way that we carry on eating McDonald's burgers. The consequences are now self-evident. Like obesity, that conditioned anti-EU sentiment has risen to the surface like a skin rash.

Brexit has exposed the subconscious of our nation. The ugly underbelly of modern England. Perhaps this was inevitable in the age of social media. Many nations are being exposed. Italy, America, India, Turkey, Brazil, Hungary. There is little to be proud of. A lot to worry about. We witness the ugliness of individuals on Facebook or Twitter. People are now part of Social Groups. Everything is polarised. All trust in the common ground is lost. These rifts, these wounds, this dirt, this excavation of our collective soul is revealing something quite sinister about the human condition. It reveals that the concentration camps, the genocides, the race riots, the class divisions, and revolutions of the past were not aberrations in our history. Humanity is not just susceptible to taking sides. We are susceptible to creating conditions for conflict. We are susceptible to becoming thugs, murders, genocidal collectively.

There is a solution. But for an alcoholic the first step is to admit that there is a problem. The first step is to confront the truth. The truths about Brexit are quite simple.

The Referendum in 2016 was an advisory referendum. People voted to Leave in a binary vote. No one knew the destination. Now we know. We embarked on the journey to leave the EU. On the way not only have we discovered unforeseen obstacles, but as we have learnt where we are likely to end up. We have analysed the consequences and determined that Brexit is an act of a great national harm. It is a self-inflicting wound where new raptures will continue to emerge for a long time to come.

The future remains unknowable. But we know that we are walking on the cliff's edge. We do not need to go it alone. We can play our part in shaping humanities destiny instead of becoming a minor player.

My personal view is that Brexit is bad for Britain. Brexit is mad for Britain. It is not in the national interest. Brexit will reduce our individual and collective outcomes. Freedom of Movement will come to an end for our children. The possibilities of life and to love and choice to live anywhere in the EU will be denied to most British people. Our world of imagination will become smaller. Or dreams will reduce.

Monumental Mistake

The argument that Tories put forward for leaving the EU is that we had a referendum. That a referendum be held was voted on by Parliament. The people delivered a mandate. Article 50 was triggered. Now we must deliver on Brexit.

All forget the lies told. They forget the promises made. They forget the illegality of Arron Banks pumping the leave campaign with £8m of funds. They forget the role of Cambridge Analytica. All they say is that the last referendum held was in 1974. Referendums are not frequent and when they happen, we must deliver.

This is same as saying that generally we do not trust the British people to vote on important issues because collectively they are not well informed and are likely to get it wrong. That is the sole purpose of having an elected chamber - the House of Parliament - to make decisions on behalf of the electorate.

What the referendum proved is that nations can make monumental mistakes. This is nothing new. Germans elected Hitler. India and England embarked on Independence without preparation. America went to war in Vietnam. Americans have elected Donald Trump. Ugandans elected Idi Amin. Gene modifications are happening without adequate oversight and regulations. AI will bring about unforeseen change.

Humanity either must live with the consequences or adjust and make changes.

The fear mongers now talk about being in 'unchartered waters' if Parliament votes down Mrs. May's deal. The No Deal option has effectively been removed by the motion put forward by Dominic Grieves, which instructs Mrs. May to come up with Plan B within 3-days if her deal is rejected. The options left then are either another deal, which we are told is not possible because the EU has stated that it is the only deal possible, or No Brexit.

'Unchartered waters' is just an expression. Memories of the Titanic. Columbus lost at sea at a time when his compass took him west when he thought he was going east. In fact, No Deal Brexit is unchartered because we don't know how the complex links between the EU and UK might break.

Mrs. May is running around to try and get more assurances from the EU on the Irish Backstop. That too is delusional, for how can the EU give way on the security of N. Ireland?

When Jeremy Hunt alluded to the possibility of No Brexit yesterday (11/01/2019), the Pound jumped from $1.2750 to $1.2840 and against the EUR from Eur 1.1085 to Eur 1.1195. Any sign that Brexit might be abandoned will result in a strong Pound and better outlook for the British economy.

The question at the time of this writing is: Will Brexit be abandoned through an act of Parliament or through a People Vote and a new referendum?

The People are held in such high regard in this great democracy. But the British populace is a semi-literate lot. Even the well to do, well informed, don't exercise their democratic rights. They see power as institutionalised and remote. Evidence of that remoteness is found on the front benches of the opposition. The Labour party's sole intent is to get into power. They don't care about the consequences on jobs or the economy, because for them that is just the cost of being in power. Labour, the Lib Dems and obviously the Tories will do or say anything to win votes.

Labour fortunately doesn't command enough votes to seek a mandate for a new General Election. Even if a GE was triggered, there is little evidence that Jeremy Corbyn's vision of Britain will win. Jeremy Corbyn and John McDonnell make lots of promises. Very few believe that they will be able to implement. This will cost Labour votes. That is probably a good thing, for Jeremy Corbyn is inflexible and may end up causing more harm than good to the British economy. Our democracy will probably lead to a coalition government. Balanced but unable to do very much.

There is so much that can be done at the sensible centre of British politics. Reverting to EU Membership may well be our only anchor of stability and sense.

*

Time has passed. It is April 24th, 2019. Brexit has not happened. Theresa May was instructed by Parliament to ask for an extension. Extension was granted by the EU. The next date is October 31, 2019. It is highly likely that UK will not get another extension after that new deadline.

Mrs. May has reached out to the opposition Labour leadership to see if a compromise can be found. This very act has made some members of her own party furious. The hardliners want to get rid of her. Today the 1922 Committee met to see if they can change the rules to force Mrs. May's resignation. The last No Confidence Vote was defeated and in theory another motion cannot be brought for 12-months. News is just out that Sir Graham Brady confirms that there is to be no change to the rules.

Newspapers suggest that Boris Johnson is planning a leadership challenge. When Boris Johnson does challenge and if he wins the leadership contest, I expect the Tory party to unravel further.

As far as one can tell the Labour leadership is not insisting on a 2nd Referendum, even though they are making noises to that effect. It is highly unlikely that the two main parties will be able to agree on a way forward. They will play games and waste time, but Thresa May is unlikely to give much ground and Jeremy and party are unlikely to budge from their own positions. However, it is possible that Brexit will still go through Parliament. The ERG and DUP may very well come together and vote for a version of Thresa May's deal. If it just scrapes though, will it last?

*

May 20th, 2019: The talks with Labour came to an end without agreement. One shouldn't say that the talks completely failed. Mrs. May is going to bring back a version of her deal with some changes for workers' rights and try and get it through Parliament in the week of June 3rd. It is unlikely to pass.

In the meantime, the contest for the leadership of the Tory Party has heated up and Mrs. May has been forced to set a date for her departure. She has agreed to setting that date after, hopefully, final attempt to agree a deal. If the Tory leadership contest ensues soon that will eat up time and again the October 31st deadline will not be met easily. Some argue that revoking Article 50 will then be the only option as No Deal Brexit has already been ruled out by Parliament. A new leader, likely to be Boris Johnson may try to push No Deal through.

Over the last few months Nigel Farage has set up the Brexit Party to participate in the EU elections. There is tremendous support for it. A huge wave of defections from the Tory Party primarily, but also from UKIP and some from Labour has taken place such that the Brexit Party is on track to winning the most seats in the European Parliament. Support for the Brexit Party is upward of 30%.

Nationalism is no longer a protest. It is a wave spreading across not only Europe, but the world. Today, Nerendra Modi will be reconfirmed to have won a second term with an absolute majority in the Indian elections. That nationalistic wave is likely to be of greater consequence compared to Brexit as India will end up being the 3rd largest economy in the world. The trade dispute between the United States and China will lead to more retrenchment. Brazil voted along nationalistic policies. Closer to home, Austria, Italy, Turkey, Poland, Hungary have increasingly become more insular.

The divisions in the UK have become so pronounced that Brexiters are not talking to Remainers. The Brexiters are willing to pay the cost of No Deal Brexit. The costs are huge and will be long lasting. These emotional waves, these patriotic waves, these desperate waves of a people left behind by successive governments are painful to witness. These are my fellow citizens, ready to self-harm, to make a vague point about their real-life challenges, and blaming a third party, the EU, for their condition.

Boris Johnson

The Tory party members have elected their new leader. Boris Johnson came out a winner by a big majority of the 150,000 members of the Tory party. Jeremy Hunt lost and has gone on holidays with his family to Portugal. Boris Johnson won by promising that come what may Britain will leave the EU on October 31st, 2019 - Deal or No Deal.

On winning, a significant number of the old Cabinet resigned or were fired. The new Cabinet consists entirely of Brexiters. Dominic Raab has been made Foreign Secretary. Priti Patel, Home Secretary, Sajid Javid has taken Phillip Hammond's job as Chancellor of the Exchequer, Steven Barclay has remained the Brexit Secretary, Michael Gove has been appointed to the post of preparing for No Deal Brexit and Jacob Rees-Mogg has been given the post of Leader of the Commons. All are now working to make Brexit happen.

The first firing shots have been to tell the EU that the Withdrawal Agreement negotiated by Mr. May is dead. The WA covers what the UK must pay the EU for its share of future liabilities. An amount of £39 billion has been agreed. The agreement also covers, among other things, citizen rights and importantly the border arrangements particularly on the island of Ireland, between the Republic of Ireland and N. Ireland. The Agreement allows for a 2-year transition period during which Brexit would be implemented. During the transition period UK would not have a voice in EU decisions but will remain part of the European Economic Area (EEA), the single market and customs unions and be subject to European Court of Justice (ECJ) laws.

The border between the Republic of Ireland and N. Ireland is the key hard border between the EU and Great Britain. The situation is complicated because the Good Friday Agreement, which brought peace in Ireland, does not permit a hard border between the Republic and N. Ireland. Free Movement of goods and people are the foundation of that peace agreement. The fear is that any interference with the Good Friday Agreement would not be acceptable as it might compromise peace. Some proposals have been made, that away from the border or even at the border, in time, there could be technology solutions where goods and possibly illegal people passing through can be screened. That technology solution is not ready and may take years to implement. Recognising this, the EU27 and UK government under Mrs. May agreed, that there can be what is termed the 'Irish backstop.' This essentially says that until a solution is available there will be no hard border. Trade flows will continue as now, and would remain subject to EU laws.

The Tory hardliners oppose the backstop because they argue that the EU can force UK to stay in the Single Market and Customs Union indefinitely. At the same time, they also insist that a hard border would not be implemented by either side as that would compromise peace. Boris Johnson does not have a solution to the backstop, but they want it to be removed from the Withdrawal Agreement. The EU has continued to insist that removing the backstop is not up for negotiations. Boris Johnson has been threatening that unless the EU gets rid of the backstop, UK will crash out.

The Withdrawal Agreement has been rejected 3 times in the House of Commons. Labour rejected it because they wanted a different type of Brexit. The hard-lined Tories have rejected it because they want to be simply out of the EU as soon as possible. Boris Johnson wants the backstop to become a problem to be solved during the transition period. The EU is saying that if there is a solution during the 2-year transition period, the need for the backstop would vanish. If there is no solution the backstop will stay.

Boris Johnson is painting an extremely optimistic picture of post Brexit Britain. Donald Trump is coaxing him along by saying that trade with the US can expand 4 to 5 folds. At the same time the US Democrats have warned that there will not be a trade deal with UK if the Irish peace process is jeopardised in any way.

*

Parliament has closed for its summer vacation. September and October promise to be intense months. No Deal Brexit stance has already pushed the Pound towards $1.20, its lowest point since 2016.

What is the economic case for Brexit?

When I lived in Hong Kong and Singapore, I was envious of these small economies. It was nearly free for all. Extremely low personal taxes, around 15-17%. Nearly full employment. Relatively well educated and large percentage of the population in the Middle Classes. Great public services -transport, roads, schools, universities. Extremely tightly regulated immigration system that brought in cheap Labour without any rights to clean and cook and serve as waiter and doormen. A low wage economy at the bottom. Truly little spending on defence, but open to trade with everyone. There were hidden taxes on consumption. Both are strategically located City States, although Hong Kong is inevitably part of greater China. On the surface everything seemed to work. Often I was thinking why should Britain not be like this? These old colonies had increased their living standards enormously while we appear to be relatively stagnant. Can we be like Hong Kong, Singapore or even Switzerland? Are low taxes and tariff free trade the answer?

The answer lies in what part of our way of life do we want to surrender. Our NHS takes about 7% of GDP. Social Security, defence, education, public services, transport etc. are our national priorities. Lower taxes mean less spending. Less spending impacts disproportionately the least well off. These are all political choices. No Deal Brexit Britain will be more and more like Hong Kong and Singapore, but with new challenges because of our geographic location. We are in Europe. The EU is the world's biggest frictionless trading block. Making our tax regime free for all, will impact the European economies as wealth will flow from the EU to the UK. It will give us an unfair advantage. EU will respond by putting up new barriers and introduce new regulations and impose new taxes. It won't work, although there is nothing to stop us from spending less on the NHS or education and so on. This will change the structure of our economy. Citizens can be given greater choice on how they spend their earnings. But that comes at the cost of leaving the most vulnerable in society exposed.

Boris Johnson's No Deal Brexit is a vision for Britain to become more unequal, more divided, more right-wing with everyone fending for themselves. In increasing income disparity, Boris Johnson is willing to make the nation poorer overall. For Boris Johnson it is the size of the slice they get, not the size of the cake. Therein lies the fantasy of No Deal Brexit. Our nation is falling for his charm and wit and clever use of language, but really the man is unbelievably bad with numbers and projections and changes his mind and views as the situation demands. Boris Johnson has no memory of his own misdemeanours. Like his many affairs, Boris Johnson leads people on, screws them and when it suits him, he ditches and leaves them behind. He will do the same with our country. The life of Boris Johnson is about Boris Johnson.

Boris Johnson's adult life has been shaped largely by his time at The Spectator and The Telegraph, both publications owned by Conrad Black and both appealing to conservative, middle England. To give him credit, he did win elections as Mayor of London and as an MP before and after, be that for safe Tory seats. He is part of the political machinery and because of his upbringing has long standing connections with people in power and in business - people who control the media and have money. A man like Boris Johnson is ideal as a leader when little leadership is required. London was literally a boom town during much of his tenure. A few popular measures won adulation from many Londoners.

Secretly the English love characters who misbehave. Whether it is Benny Hill or Morecombe and Wise, we like our naughty scandalous boys and unfaithful husbands. Their secret wish is to be like the characters of East Enders where every adult male and female have slept with nearly everybody else. In this sense Boris Johnson has been very astute. He knows how to be popular. Abusing the weak, making fun of foreigners, mixing a little bit of hate mongering, and keeping a distance and pretending to be upper crust goes down well with the English. His popularity is well earned and deserved.

Boris Johnson is not a man for detail and problem solving. He is more of a problem maker. Any agreement with the EU must be practical, detailed, and complex. Asking Boris Johnson to master complexity is like asking a monkey to understand and write down the equations for the theory of relativity. So, what does a man who has oversold himself throughout his life do? He waves his hands and refuses to address the issues at hand and tries to find short-cuts. Short cuts that are unrealistic and unworkable.

This is where we now find ourselves. Boris Johnson has given the EU a unilateral ultimatum to remove the Irish backstop from the Withdrawal Agreement or face a No Deal exit on October 31st. He has threatened that Britain would leave the EU without a deal and with no arrangements in place for the future relationship. The EU, for its part, has asked that the UK government come back with a viable, alternative workable arrangement. As of today (01/09/2019) no alternative has been presented.

There appears to be a wide consensus in Parliament that Britain should not leave the EU without a deal. But that Parliament majority requires the defection of Tory MPs. Boris Johnson fears that his No Deal Brexit threats will be taken away by Parliament. Given the prospect of this opposition, Boris Johnson asked the Queen last week to shut down Parliament from end of next week to 14th of October with the excuse of holding a Queens Speech on the agenda of the 'new' government. The Queen has consented. This action of *proroguing* Parliament is seen as undemocratic and a possible way of forcing through No Deal Brexit, without Parliaments consent.

The opposition parties have come together, with support from some Conservative MPs, and they have agreed that starting on Tuesday, Parliament will try to pass legislation to prevent No Deal Brexit, by making leaving the EU without a deal unlawful. Parliament has only 4 days to pass these bills by both chambers. If the bills do not become law before the Queen formally shuts down Parliament, then the possibility of Britain leaving the EU without a deal becomes real.

There have been huge demonstrations across Britain against Boris Johnson trying to shut down Parliament. It is likely that the government will ignore these protests and press ahead. This week will be decisive in the story of Brexit. There are legal challenges in the High Court in Scotland as well as an action being brought about by Gina Miller and the former Prime Minister John Major. The speaker of House of Commons, John Bercow has described the move by Boris Johnson as 'A constitutional outrage.'

The stakes are extremely high. If No Deal is stopped in its tracks by law, Boris Johnson is likely to call a snap general election. The date for the election could be set for early November. Again, that is after the date of extension. Unless Article 50 is withdrawn, or the EU agrees to a further extension at the request of the PM, then Britain will crash out of the EU with dire consequences. Parliament must do its job so that any manoeuvrings by the government to crash Britain out is prevented.

We are living in dangerous times. The forces behind the drive to exit the EU are complex and mysterious. A new alignment of Britain with the United States must be the aim of the far-right Conservative Party. Why a closer relationship between the US and the whole of Europe is not in the best interest of the US, one cannot easily comprehend. Is the driving force behind Brexit, Trump's America wanting to take over the UK economy?

With Britain becoming just another country, just another medium sized economy, is greatness only going to be possible by becoming the 52nd State of the United States? Is American takeover desirable? While the English may be happy quitting the EU, the Scots, the Irish and increasingly the Welsh want to remain. Why are the Brexiters willing to see the breakup of the United Kingdom?

Brexiters are acting as if they were in a cult. National harm and self-harm are not dissuading them. These ruptures in Britain will not heal for a generation, no matter what happens on November 1st. Reconciliation is only possible by holding a new referendum where the British people decide on the terms of our departure (a deal) or No Deal verses the option of keeping what we have - Remain. My personal fear is that even a 2nd Referendum will not heal the wounds and for a long time the nation will remain divided.

Some people say that we are living in interesting times. If interesting is seeing the ruptures in our national psyche, then perhaps these are interesting times. It is rare to see nations expose themselves collectively to such high risks. Only in times of war or committing genocide do nations plunder national wealth. I personally do not find what I am seeing attractive. My assumptions about the actions of an advanced human society requires serious reassessment. We could be on the verge of a civil war. I find nothing interesting about chaos, uncertainty and observing the collective madness of our people. It is disheartening and sad. It is as if each day something is dying in each one of us and there is not anything we can do to contain the damage.

This is a good place to end my observations on English Brexit. A last Chapter perhaps at the conclusion of the negotiations with the EU, when we shall know what kind of Deal Boris Johnson's government has been able to agree with our biggest trading partners.

The long-term future takes care of itself.

COVID-19 & The Failure of Government

I must have been among the first residents of Europe to get Covid-19. In January we went to a Chinese restaurant in Zurich. I was speaking to a man of around 40 who had just come back from China. A few days later I was bed ridden. I had the worst form of illness imaginable. I could hardly breathe. My temperature fluctuated wildly. My body felt heavy and my muscles ached. I had no strength. It lasted nearly two weeks and recovery was then slow. I thought I was going to die. Contracting Covid-19 was the worst illness of my 65-years of living.

Only a couple of weeks later stories of the infection in Wuhan and then in Italy started to make daily news. Stories also of how China was reacting to the virus and where it might have originated. Reporters spoke of live markets. The scientific community is in consensus that the transmission of the virus is from animals to humans. Obviously, it can pass on from human to human when contracted.

I have been to China, Taiwan, Hong Kong, and South Korea. The conditions in which they keep live animals and their culinary habits of killing the animals just before slicing and cooking. Prawns, fish, crabs are packaged alive for people to take away to throw on grills or boiling water. The sight of what is on offer in these markets is difficult to watch, without thinking just how cruel these people are.

I am not religious. But from childhood, I have been touched by the suffering of animals in captivity. What one sees in China in these markets is comparable to what one sees in a bullring in Spain. The capacity of man to inflict suffering on other species has no bounds.

Covid-19 had spread from Wuhan to Italy, Switzerland. Everyone knew that it would reach Britain. The response from Boris Johnson and his advisor Dominic Cummings was to do nothing. The initial response was to allow the virus to spread and allow what they call 'herd immunity' to develop. Questions were being asked as to how many deaths are acceptable to keep the economy going. China went into a lockdown.

The news of stringent lockdown in Wuhan, China and the efforts being made by the authorities were being broadcasted each day. The number of cases and daily casualties were being released. We were astonished by the scale and speed with which China organised to contain the virus. We were not surprised that the Chinese people cooperated and followed the guidelines to self-isolate and wear masks. While our attention was on China, a country far away, Covid-19 had already travelled to Europe as cases started to emerge in Italy and then Spain. The whole of Northern Italy was shut down as the death toll started to increase. We knew that the virus would come to Britain. Boris Johnson just waited for it.

WHO declared Covid-19 as a Public Health Emergency of International Concern on 30th of January and a pandemic on March 11, 2020.

The first response from the government was to do nothing. Dominic Cummings and thus Boris Johnson had decided that the economic cost of lockdown was too high a price. They did their calculations and concluded that a certain (uncertain) number of deaths was a price worth paying. They assumed that so called herd Immunity to the virus would be achieved in no time and thought they could allow the whole population to be inflected. Voices from the scientific community and particularly that of Professor Ian Ferguson from Imperial College dispelled the notion. Professor Ferguson estimated death toll rising to as much as 500,000 in the UK unless the government introduced strict lockdown measures. Those measures were finally introduced in March 2020 as the NHS was starting to be overwhelmed by the number of new cases and the rising number of deaths. The most vulnerable were the old, obese, Asians, blacks and generally people with health conditions such as diabetes.

Covid-19 infection rates started to be reported from February 2020. The actual number of infections were probably already much higher than recorded numbers. People simply were not being tested. But as soon as records started to be published and people started to visit their GPs the numbers quickly increased until a month or so later four to five thousand cases were being reported each day. There were signs that if the trend continued the NHS would be overwhelmed. In March, the government introduced the first nationwide lockdown using the words 'Stay Home, Protect the NHS, Save Lives.' People with symptoms were asked to self-isolate.

Donald Trump, in America, similarly did not want to acknowledge the virus or take it seriously. He started to blame China for its spread and started to call it the 'China Virus.' He started to dismiss the virus by saying it will weaken in warm weather. Then he said, it will just disappear, like a miracle. Despite the rising number of cases, Trump continued to say that the virus will go away or that there wouldn't be so many deaths. Trump also didn't encourage people to wear masks. Many Americans still think that wearing a mask is against their civil liberties. On the campaign trail, Trump held rallies where his supporters were not wearing masks. The result is that more than 300,000 Americans have died from Covid-19 to date. At the time of writing, around 3,000 Americans are dying every day from the virus.

Americans lost 20 million jobs from February to April 2020 directly from the shutdown of the hospitality sector. Responses to the virus were left to governors of each state. Republicans states took much less drastic measures compared with democratic ones and allowed more people to die from Covid. Perhaps it was their way of inflicting casualties on the most vulnerable communities - the blacks or Latinos who are generally living in bigger family units.

Boris Johnson is only slightly less of an idiot compared with Donald Trump. Only when it became apparent that the rising number of cases would mean that more and more patients will have to be admitted to hospitals until all the capacity of the NHS would be used up, did the government start to take the virus seriously. In that sense we have been lucky. Because NHS services are free and must be provided by law. There was no escape from these obligations.

Great Britain simply was not ready to cope with a pandemic. Many countries had developed software to trace the spread of the virus from reported cases. Technology exists to try and identify people who might have been in close contact with someone who has caught to virus. They can then be contacted and asked to self-isolate. Under Matt Hancock, our health secretary, it has been an exercise in incompetence. Our systems have taken three times as long to start functioning.

To safeguard our medical staff, the government had to order Personal Protection Equipment (PPE) - facemasks, gloves, gowns that would protect staff while they treated patients. There are so many stories of this government handing out contracts to friends to supply or intermediate purchase of PPE through newly established companies with the sole purpose of collecting commissions. Our government has spent more than GBP 12 billion on purchases. That is estimated to be billions more than what was needed to be spent. Perhaps the extent of corruption will be revealed one day. For politicians, the misuse of public money to enrich themselves or their friends is not a new political strategy. Alas, this is not new.

In many states in America and in England the lockdowns were relaxed way too early. It was as if a child requiring three doses of medicine, not liking the taste, decided not to take the full course. The virus came back in what was described as the second wave. Now we are facing the third wave.

Large segments of the American and British of populations have turned the pandemic into a political issue. Unintelligent people simply have failed to grasp that the virus does not understand politics or our sense of freedom. It simply infects when given the chance. When infected a percentage end up dying.

In Britain, a disproportionate percentage of blacks and Asians work in public services - nurses, doctors, pharmacists, dentists, bus drivers etc. This segment has suffered the most from Covid-19 not only because they are the so called 'front line' workers but also because a greater percentage live in extended families or have medical conditions that compromise their immune systems. Perhaps it is the daily exposure to the sick in hospitals that results in weakened immunity.

We have lost more than 3 million jobs. The High Street has been decimated as only essential shops, food and pharmacies could remain open. On the other hand, lockdown has accelerated all business linked to the 'stay at home' economy. Online service providers such as Amazon, Microsoft, Netflix, Ocado, Zoom Video and Gaming companies' shares have gone through the roof. Remote working, automation the PPE manufacturers and pharmaceutical companies have also fared well. Millions of workers across the developed countries were given financial help. Governments thought that the pandemic will be over by the end of summer 2020. It is not over.

As people were forced to shut business Rishi Sunak, the chancellor, came up with a Furlough Scheme under which 80% of the wages of those asked to stay at home was paid up to a maximum of £2000 per month. The scale of financial support has been unprecedented. The assumption was that the spread of the virus would be contained, and things would return to normal.

Within weeks many companies and University research labs started to disclose that they already had developed or were close to developing vaccines. Fast approvals were given to start clinical trials. An American company, Moderna, became prominent by declaring that they had a vaccine that would be ready within months. It quickly raised over $600m of new money, valuing the company at over $7billion. In the last 6 month the market capitalisation of Moderna has jumped to over $50 billion. Moderna's Covid-19 vaccine is based on mRNA technology. The vaccine has been approved. Distribution has started. Gilead Science Inc. made claims that its existing drug, branded Ramdesivir was effective in reducing infection severity. Gilead shares also jumped on the news. The share price has since fallen back because a study by WHO has shown that Ramdesivir is not effective against Covid-19. Russia has approved a drug named, Sputnik V. Cambridge University, Oxford University/AstraZeneca, Johnson & Johnson, a German Company BioNTech/Pfizer and many others have been developing vaccines. Some have been approved.

Vaccinations on large scale have begun. But given the number that must be inoculated it will take at least 6 months to a year to immunise populations. The poor countries will face big hurdles because vaccine supplies have already been purchased by the rich nations and their healthcare infrastructure remains underdeveloped. There is no alternative, other than to neutralise the virus across the globe. Unless this is done, it will continue to wreak havoc.

For Great Britain, the divisiveness of the nation over Brexit has been muted by Covid-19. The news cycle focused on the spread of the virus and the resulting struggles of the NHS and near 70,000 deaths. Great Britain has been one of the worst performers on almost every score. The reason is that we have probably, like Trump's America, the most incompetent Prime Minister and Cabinet in the history.

No deal is not an option

Early Parliamentary General Election Act 2019 was passed with 428 to 20 votes for the election to be held on December 12, 2019. The Conservatives won by a majority of 80 seats by decimating Labour in many of its key area. Boris Johnson ran the election with a slogan, 'Get Brexit Done,' a phrase coined by Dominic Cummings, the Chief Advisor to Boris Johnson.

Jeremy Corbyn and his shadow chancellor, John McDonnell threw every inducement at the working classes. Free education, free transport for under 18-year olds, free childcare, end to homelessness, free this, free that, free everything. In the end, no one believed that Jeremy Corbyn would be able to deliver on the promises he was making. On top of that allegations of anti-Semitism against the Labour Party and Jeremy Corbyn's inability to deal with it cost a lot of votes. Labour lost 60 seats. Jeremey Corbyn resigned, and Keir Stammer, the more centrist politician became the new leader of the Labour Party. The Liberal Democrats, under Jo Swinson gained, overall, more votes, but lost one seat. Jo Swinson was voted out. Jo resigned and Ed Davey was elected as the new leader.

Unsurprisingly, the emotional idea that the British people wanted to be in control and masters of their own destiny took hold. We want our sovereignty back. We want to make our own rules. We will set even higher environmental standards and the promises to level up, meaning that more investment would be directed to the North and more power would be given to the regions had a big impact. The English do have faith in themselves. 'We will prosper, no matter what!' Many treated Brexit like warfare. It was as if they were personally being imprisoned by the rules and regulations of the EU and had to liberate themselves.

The SNP, with Nicola Sturgeon as leader won 48 out of 59 seats in Scotland – a gain of 13 seats. In Northern Ireland, the pro EU, nationalists, SDLP and Alliance won seats from the DUP and gained a majority.

With an 80-seat majority Boris Johnson was given a free hand to run the country as he pleases for the next four years. All the key posts were given to Brexiters. Priti Patel was made Home Secretary. Sajid Javid retained his position as Chancellor but was soon replaced by Rishi Sunak. Dominic Raab was made Foreign Secretary. Lis Truss was made Secretary for International Trade. Lord David Frost was assigned the role of Chief Negotiator on Brexit.

Behind the scenes they have made progress in the negotiations. But contentious issues remain on which the gap still has not been closed. Frequent threats by Lord Frost, the chief British negotiator with the European Commission and Boris Johnson that Britain is willing to walk away with a No Deal have been a recurring theme. The two main issues on which there is still no agreement are State Aid and Fisheries.

Fish accounts for less than 0.04% of UKs GDP. But it is a question of pride that UK should be able to control who and to what extent foreigners can fish in UK waters, even though much of the fish that is caught ends up being sold to EU countries. From the side of the EU, a lot of jobs and lives depend on fishing in British waters. If we deny them a access, the countries of the EU may ban fish caught by British boats to be sold in the EU or put big tariffs on such trade. Trade agreements are, by definition, compromises on sovereignty.

State Aid issue is simple. To have a level playing field in trade, the EU and its members have agreements in place that monitor how much public funds can be used to support industry. Clearly if the UK provides 'free money' to support industry and jobs, those industries can also then sell their products at a loss and gain market share. In an economic zone that that has free movement of people, goods and services giving selected industries or sectors special treatment through State Aid makes a mockery of competition. Britain still has a plethora of legacy industries such as Ship Building, Steel Manufacturing and even Auto Manufacturing which are hopelessly uncompetitive. The cost of vast numbers being unemployed are far greater compared to the State Aid that needs to be given to keep these industries ticking over, without making profits. Used properly State Aid could be a tool to buy time and be a lifeline to many desperate communities facing challenges of global competition. Apparently, Liz Truss has signed a trade deal with Japan in which rules on State Aid have been agreed that are more restrictive compared to what we are willing to agree with the EU.

A level playing field in area of taxation can also end up being uncompetitive. The arguments used by the Tories is that if we are leaving the EU, then we must be treated as a Sovereign State. Frequently the point is made that GB should be treated same as the EU treats Canada or Australia. The EU response is that if we want to be treated like Australia in some respects, then why not in all respects? Australia does not have a Free Trade Agreement with the EU. Trade happens on World Trade Organisation Rules. WTO rules impose significant tariffs on traded good.

*

As I write (15/12/2020) the day of reckoning is approaching. No meaningful progress had been made until last week. Yesterday Boris Johnson met with the President of the EU, Ursula Von Der Leyen. Apparently, Boris Johnson tried to suggest that the EU fire its chief negotiator, Michel Barnier. Ursula supposedly told Johnson that Mr. Barnier has the full support of the EU. Boris then tried to arrange a call/meeting with Emmanuel Macron, the French President and Angela Merkle, the German Chancellor. Both refused because the EU has handed over the responsibility for Brexit negotiations to the European Commission.

Despite Boris Johnson saying that there is a greater possibility of No Deal and that an Australian style trading arrangement (which is same as No Deal) is what we will end up with, the negotiations have been extended.

No Deal is not an option simply because neither the UK nor the EU are prepared to handle a No Deal scenario. No Deal implies border controls, implementation of tariffs. That is a lot of paperwork. 97% of the deal has been agreed already. It has taken 3 years. The outstanding issues will need to be resolved sooner or later. The only problem is that the extreme right wing of the Tory party is delusional about Britain's prospects and want a 'clean' break. There is no break from our biggest trading partner, the EU. Britain cannot go it alone.

The British economy has been the worst performer among the G7 during 2020. Due primarily to Covid-19. No Deal Brexit will take further significant toll on jobs and living standards. The EU has announced emergency measure allowing airline to fly, fishermen to fish for another year, and trucks to cross the borders.

The stark reality is that Britain is the junior partner in these negotiations. We can make all the noises we want, but one can see that with Ursula Von Der Leyen, Boris Johnson is like a child. Now that Joe Biden is going to be the next President of the United States, Britain also doesn't have allies. The EU was our great friend. The EU was always more special compared to the United States. It is a sad fact that Britain prefers to be treated like a little puppy by the Americans instead of being treated as an equal by the EU countries.

Joe Biden has sent clear signals to this Tory government that a US/UK trade deal is not on the top of his agenda. Deal with Covid-19 is his top priority.

No deal is also not an option because if on the 1st of January 2021 we have to revert to trading on WTO terms, then on the same day discussions will restart to negotiate better terms.

*

A deal was agreed on the 24th December 2020. The costs will now start to be counted. The costs of taking away individual freedoms will be extremely hard to compute. How does one estimate the cost of missed opportunities?

The Deal agreed required the junior partner, UK to compromise on Fishing. For the next five and half years, EU will retain fishing rights. UK was seeking 80% reduction. We'll get 25% reduction in EU quota. The EU will compensate its fisheries.

On the level playing field, the UK has compromised. A framework will be setup to monitor if the playing field is not level. If found not be level, either side can impose tariffs.

The Service Sector was not properly addressed. UK will lose Passporting rights from December 31st, 2020. The concept of 'equivalence' is framework that will be followed thereafter. Equivalence will result in the UK conforming to EU laws and regulations for the financial services sector.

The end

19/12/2020

Postscript

Brexit is done. The whole reason for Brexit was to be able to control the influx of immigrants. Instead of Free Movement from within the EU, the Tory party wants to implement a Points based system, such that only skilled and educated workers will be allowed entry.

The pandemic has proven above all that the line between lower paid workers, who are usually labelled unskilled, and those with higher education, is a blur. Bus drivers, nurses, cleaners, teachers, garbage collectors, construction workers, food or parcel delivery workers, uber drivers etc. are as important to the functioning of an efficient economy as bankers, professors, politicians, architects and doctors. All services are essential, particularly the front-line staff who put their lives at risk. EU immigration has indeed fallen over the last couple of years. In part that could also be because UK economy has underperformed. Still the UK economy remains short of all types of skills. The result has been that immigration from non-EU countries has risen.

If we want to reduce immigration we have to train and educate our citizens to meet the evolving requirements of the economy.

A skills-based immigration system has its own flaws. The more educated foreigners will in time rise to the highest ranks in the economy. The foreigner hating Brexiters won't like working under their supervision. They will not benefit from the richness of the cultures that foreigners bring, that is often imparted in the school playground. They will remain marginalised waving their little flags.

If Covid-19 has proven one thing, it is that we all live under the same sky and stars. We are all susceptible to the spread of diseases. Viruses don't recognise national boundaries. Both the Moderna vaccine and BioNTech's were developed by businesses set up by first-generation immigrants.

The murder of George Floyd in Minneapolis showed that racism remains a big challenge in America. The protests lead by the BlackLivesMatter movement showed that humanity can come together to counter the, virus like, spread of nationalism. Humanities greatest challenges are global. We all need to come together to tackle Climate Change, reduction in biodiversity, pollution, and global inequality.

Brexit wasted four and half years. Brexit will have hardly any discernible benefits. The United Kingdom is on the brink of breaking up. Remainers and Brexiters live in alternatives realities. The divisions, the reduced economic outcomes for our citizens will have repercussions for decades to come.

The only thing that Brexit has made visible is the enormous amount of hate that burdens at least 52% of our people.

I am not hopeful that hate will be contained in the English culture.